## Advance Praise for *Focus*

"For leaders and managers of people, this is *must reading*: it's like finding the missing link in human evolution or the Rosetta Stone in language translation."

—Ken Shelton, editor of *Leadership Excellence* magazine

"*Focus* is an engaging, highly practical guide that makes complex ideas at the forefront of motivational science accessible to a wide audience, offering surprising insights and applications for dealing more effectively with everyday work and life challenges. It will be an eye-opener for people who thought they understood motivation."

—Walter Mischel, past president of the Association for Psychological Science

"How do we actually motivate people to disrupt or drive change? In their eye-opening book *Focus*, social scientists Heidi Grant Halvorson and Tory Higgins provide a comprehensive tool kit for motivating yourself and those you lead."

—Whitney Johnson, *Harvard Business Review* contributor and author of *Dare, Dream, Do: Remarkable Things Happen When You Dare to Dream*

"*Focus* is a clear and engaging tour of central ideas in the study of motivation. Written by Tory Higgins, one of the world's leading experts on the topic, together with Heidi Grant Halvorson, it provides a powerful lens for understanding what makes friends, bosses, coworkers, and spouses tick. After you read it, your relations with other people will never be the same."

—Barry Schwartz, author of *The Paradox of Choice* and *Practical Wisdom* (with Kenneth Sharpe)

"Why do some people succeed at attaining goals, and others do not? Why do some products sell, whereas others lie on the shelf? *Focus* addresses these questions (and many more) in a deeply thoughtful, highly practical, and completely engaging way. This book is necessary reading for anyone interested in the fundamentals of persuasion and motivation."

—Jennifer Aaker, General Atlantic Professor of Marketing at Stanford University, author of *The Dragonfly Effect*

"This great book makes science fun—providing an empowering look at evidence-based research on how to optimize our motivational focus. It's packed with big ideas that give us insight into how we can apply this wisdom to all aspects of our lives."

—Brian Johnson, founder and CEO of the en*theos Academy for Optimal Living

"*Focus* is brilliant. Two of the leading researchers on success and motivation, Heidi Grant Halvorson and Tory Higgins, have teamed up to give us an extraordinary gift of clear thinking, clever writing, and enjoyable reading about a topic of vital concern to all of us—what drives our thinking, our choices, and our actions. It's an absolutely fascinating read, and I learned more from this book than from any other I've read in a long, long time. And so will you. *Focus* is full of stunning insights, illuminating examples, practical advice, and solid and surprising research. It's a fascinating new perspective on motivation, and it has lessons in it for managers, parents, teachers, coaches, students, researchers, writers, coworkers . . . even film buffs and romantics. Buy this book and gain a whole new perspective on your life, your work, your family, and your community. It is that good."

—Jim Kouzes, coauthor of the bestselling *The Leadership Challenge* and the Dean's Executive Fellow of Leadership, Leavey School of Business, Santa Clara University

# FCUS

Use Different Ways of
Seeing the World for
Success and Influence

Heidi Grant Halvorson, Ph.D.
E. Tory Higgins, Ph.D.

HUDSON
STREET
PRESS

HUDSON STREET PRESS

Published by the Penguin Group
Penguin Group (USA) Inc., 375 Hudson Street
New York, New York 10014, USA

USA | Canada | UK | Ireland | Australia | New Zealand | India | South Africa | China
Penguin Books Ltd, Registered Offices: 80 Strand, London WC2R 0RL, England
For more information about the Penguin Group visit penguin.com

First published by Hudson Street Press, a member of Penguin Group (USA) Inc., 2013

HUDSON REGISTERED TRADEMARK—MARCA REGISTRADA
STREET
PRESS

LIBRARY OF CONGRESS CATALOGING-IN-PUBLICATION DATA

Halvorson, Heidi Grant-,1973-
    Focus : use different ways of seeing the world for success and influence / Heidi Grant Halvorson and E. Tory Higgins.
      p. cm.
    Includes bibliographical references and index.
    ISBN 978-1-59463-102-3
  1. Motivation (Psychology)   2. Attention.   3. Success.   I. Higgins, E. Tory (Edward Tory), 1946-   II. Title.
    BF503.H346 2013
    153.8–dc23
    2012033311

Printed in the United States of America
10  9  8  7  6  5  4  3  2  1

Set in Fairfield Light
Designed by Eve L. Kirch

ALWAYS LEARNING                                                                                          PEARSON

*To our family members, past and present, who shaped how we see and deal with life, and to our Motivation Science Center family, for the joy and privilege of working with you.*

# CONTENTS

# Part Two. Motivational Fit

# INTRODUCTION

Weekly meetings at Columbia University's Motivation Science Center have always been entertaining as well as instructive— and not merely because our research topic, *why people do the things they do*, is more fun to think about than, say, *advances in actuarial accounting*. Our subterranean conference room is stuffed with chairs that surround a long table, often covered with papers, drinks, and snack foods. Our chalkboards are filled with badly drawn diagrams and graphs (some that we've been talking about for months). Each week, one brave soul presents his or her work to the rest of the group, to field tough questions and receive feedback . . . sometimes complimentary, sometimes critical, often humorous.

While each of us at the center has his or her own quirks—our own habits of (long-winded) speech and (not particularly well-thought-out) dress—when it comes to how we *work*, we break down quite clearly into two general camps. (As it happens, most people in every workplace, classroom, or community on the planet belong to one of these two camps.) The distinction between the two camps can best be illustrated by introducing you to two of our most entertaining (and strong-willed) colleagues, whose names we have changed to protect the innocent (ourselves): Jon and Ray.

Jon is the kind of person that some people might call "difficult," though probably he (and we) would prefer the term "skeptic." It is a challenge to get to the end of a sentence in Jon's presence without having him interrupt you to tell you how the beginning of it was all wrong. He is immaculate in his appearance, chooses his words with precision, and never procrastinates. He is, by nature, a pessimist (the defensive kind that we describe later)—try to tell him things are going to work out just fine and watch as he gets visibly uncomfortable with your reckless and naïve attitude.

At this point, Jon is probably starting to sound a little annoying to work with, and there is no denying that he can be on occasion. But once you have gotten to know him, it's easy to see *why* he works the way he does—he is *determined* not to make mistakes. In fact, just the idea of making a mistake upsets him. (Did we mention that much of the time he is at least a little anxious? He is.) As a result, his work is usually flawless—the arguments clearly articulated and elaborately backed up with past research, the statistics so perfectly executed that they would make that actuarial accountant we mentioned earlier smile in admiration. When he criticizes our work, he does so with the genuine intention of helping us make it mistake-free. His input isn't always easy to hear, but we are always better off for having heard it.

Ray is Jon's polar opposite—the Anti-Jon. We're not sure that Ray has ever actually *worried* about anything. He is just as smart, and just as motivated, but he goes about his work (and his life) with a relentless optimism that is impossible not to envy. He doesn't sweat the small stuff—he's all about the Next Big Idea. But sometimes that sweat-free existence leads to trouble. He has been forced to label most of his possessions "If found, call Ray 555-8797" because he is always forgetting where he left them. While every other second-year PhD student prepared a PowerPoint presentation for their master's research, complete with every conceivable bell and whistle, Ray's talk consisted of two overhead slides and a Post-it Note. (It was, incidentally, one of the most impressive theses that year in terms of ideas, if not style.)

Ray's work is creative and innovative—he's not afraid to go down untraveled paths and take intellectual risks, even though some of them end up being time-wasting dead ends. But appearance-wise . . . well, Jon once remarked during a lab meeting that Ray's shirt was so wrinkled it looked like he had been keeping it in his pants pocket all morning. Maintenance is not Ray's thing.

On the surface, Jon and Ray are two talented, hardworking individuals who have the same goal: to be an outstanding scientist. When you want to influence someone else—whether you are a psychologist, manager, marketer, teacher, or parent—you usually start by trying to figure out what that person *wants* and then use that knowledge to understand and predict their behavior. But if Jon and Ray want the same thing, then why is *everything* about the way they pursue it so different?

We all know that people want good things—good products, ideas, and experiences—and they want to avoid bad ones. It would be nice for psychologists (and managers, marketers, teachers, and parents) if that was all we needed to know about motivation—if motivation were that simple. But it isn't. To understand Jon and Ray, and human beings more generally, we begin with an insight that one of us (Higgins) had over twenty years ago: there are *two fundamentally different kinds of good (and kinds of bad)*.[1]

## Two Kinds of Good (and Bad): Promotion and Prevention

People like Ray, as the old song goes, "accentuate the positive." They see their goals as opportunities for *gain* or *advancement*. In other words, they are focused on all the great things that will happen for them when they succeed—the benefits and rewards. They "play to win." When people pursue this kind of "good," we call it having a *promotion focus*. Studies from our lab (and many other labs now) show that promotion-focused people respond best to optimism and praise, are more likely to take chances and seize opportunities, and excel at creativity and innovation. Unfortunately, all that chance taking and positive thinking makes them more prone to error, less likely to completely think things through, and usually unprepared with a plan B in case things fail. For a promotion-focused person, what's *really* "bad" is a *nongain*: a chance not taken, a reward unearned, a failure to advance. They would rather say Yes! and have it blow up in their faces than feel like they let Opportunity's knock go unanswered.

Others, like Jon, tend to see their goals as opportunities to *meet* their responsibilities and to stay safe. They consider what might go badly if they don't work hard enough to achieve. They don't play to win—they play to *not lose*. They want, more than anything else, to feel secure. When people pursue this kind of "good," they have what we call a *prevention focus*. In our studies, we find the prevention-focused to be more driven by criticism and the looming possibility of failure (if, for example, they don't work hard enough) than by applause and a sunny outlook. Prevention-focused people are often more conservative and don't take chances, but their work is also more thorough, accurate, and carefully planned. Of course, if there is too much caution and hypervigilance for error, it can pretty much kill off any potential for growth, creativity, and innovation. But for the prevention-focused, the ultimate "bad" is a *loss* you failed to stop: a mistake made, a punishment received, a danger you failed to avoid. They would much prefer to say No! to an opportunity, rather than end up in hot water. Whoever first said "the devil you know is better than the one you don't" would have earned Jon's enthusiastic approval.

The members of the Motivation Science Center (or MSC, as we'll abbreviate it from now on), as well as many other labs around the world, have been hard at work for twenty years, exploring the causes and consequences of promotion and prevention focus in every aspect of our lives. We know that while everyone is concerned with *both* promotion and prevention, most people have a dominant motivational focus—the one they use to approach most of life's challenges and demands. It's also true that focus can be situation-specific: some people are promotion focused at work, but more focused on prevention when it comes to their kids. *Everyone* is promotion-focused when they line up for a lottery ticket and prevention-focused when they line up for a flu shot.

Hundreds of studies after that initial insight, it's become clear that the kind of "good" you are pursuing affects everything about you—what you pay attention to, what you value, the strategies you choose to use (and which ones actually *work* for you), and how you feel when you succeed or fail. It affects your strengths and your weaknesses, both personally and professionally. It affects how you manage your employees and how you parent your children (and why your spouse's decisions and preferences can seem so odd). Without exaggeration, your focus affects just about *everything*.

In part 1 of this book, we'll explain the nature of the promotion and prevention focuses and how they work, and you will come to understand yourself and the people around you in a whole new way. Some things will *make sense* that never did before. You'll finally see why it's so hard to be good with both the big ideas *and* the details. Why the "spontaneous" one in any couple usually isn't the one who balances the checkbook. Why you either underestimate how long everything will take or overestimate how difficult it will be—and why someone different from you can seem so strange. You'll understand the choices you've made, the experiences you are drawn to, and why you tend to prefer one brand of product to another. And you'll be able to use that knowledge to enhance your well-being and be more effective in your life.

## Increase Your Influence

It will be especially valuable for you to understand promotion and prevention if you are in the business of influencing others—if a big part of what you do every day involves informing, persuading, and motivating. (Note that this definition of "influence" applies to teachers, coaches, and parents as much as it does to marketers, managers, and advocates. Come to think of it, most of us—in one way or another—are engaged in the "business" of influence. Unless you live alone on a desert island, in which case you can try using this book to break open your coconuts.)

Products, activities, and ideas can appeal to either promotion or prevention motivation, depending on the kind of "good" or "bad" they focus on. Some are obvious: seat belts, home security systems, and mammograms are essentially about avoiding loss (*prevention focus*), while vacation homes, lottery tickets, and facelifts are about potential gains (*promotion focus*). Other products can satisfy either promotion *or* prevention motivation, depending on how you talk about them. When toothpaste is about a "whiter smile" and "fresh breath," it's a promotion-focused product. But when it's about "avoiding cavities and gingivitis," it's all about prevention.

As the studies we share with you in part 2 will show, you can learn to *speak the motivational language* of the person you are trying to influence. When you tailor your message (or their experience) to match their focus—the kind of "good" they want—they will *feel right* about it. We call this experience motivational *fit*, and we know from over a decade of research that it creates increased trust, believability, engagement, and value. Messages and experiences that are a mismatch, on the other hand, don't create motivational fit—they feel wrong and fall flat (and unfortunately, this happens all too often). To understand what we mean, let's turn our attention to the issue of "safe sex" and try to understand when using a condom will *fit* and when it won't.

## The Case of Condoms

Here's a paradox for you: why do condom sales go up in a bad economy, despite the fact that anxiety about finances reliably leads people to have *less* sex? The answer isn't as obvious as you may think. Yes, it's true that in a bad economy people are less inclined to want to have more children to support—but if wanting to avoid an unwanted pregnancy were enough, all by itself, to get people to use condoms, you'd expect them to be used *far* more frequently and reliably in a good economy, too.

Once again, it comes down to a question of motivational fit. In good times, sex is fundamentally about pleasure—it's about fun. (Or at least it's supposed to be.) Using condoms is not a good fit (no pun intended) for sex because they are not a means to pleasure—they are a means to *safety*. And as you'll see, means that work for one focus are generally awful for the other. So if at the moment when you're deciding whether to use a condom, condoms don't fit your focus, it won't *feel right* to use one.

Unless, of course, times are bad rather than good. When the economy is bad, you experience a lot of anxiety every day, and that feeling spills over into your sex life as well. Even if sex itself remains mostly about pleasure, *life* in a bad economy becomes much more about safety and security. Condoms are a great means for those goals, so they create more motivational fit with people's general focus, and using a condom starts to feel right.

## A Practical Guide

This book is a practical guide to understanding and working *with* your promotion or prevention focus. Use this knowledge in your own life, and you'll be more effective in reaching your goals. Use it as a tool to influence others, and it's as if you can create trust, value, and better performance *out of thin air*. It's like magic. Only it's real.

# PART ONE

# PROMOTION AND PREVENTION

# CHAPTER 1

# Focused on the Win, or Avoiding the Loss?

People want to be successful. They want to buy things and do things that will make them feel good and more effective. But, as we've learned from our MSC colleagues Jon and Ray, their motivation can take two very different forms—it can be focused on hanging on to what they *already have*, or on getting *even more*. *Promotion focus* is about maximizing gains and avoiding missed opportunities. We are promotion focused, like the optimistic and idea-oriented Ray, whenever our actions are driven by the desire to make progress, to stand out, to fulfill aspirations or receive accolades.

*Prevention focus*, on the other hand, is about minimizing losses, to keep things working. We are prevention focused, like the cautious and detail-oriented Jon, whenever we are trying to stay safe and secure, avoid mistakes, fulfill our duties and responsibilities, and be seen as reliable and steadfast.

How you experience the world around you—what you pay attention to, how you interpret it, and how much you care about it—will be determined to a large degree by your motivational focus at that moment. In this chapter, we dig a little deeper into the promotion and prevention motivations, explain why they exist, and describe how we are affected when we embrace each focus in the course of our everyday lives.

## Why Two Kinds of Focus?

Human beings come preprogrammed with two basic needs, each of which has to be satisfied if they are to survive: the need for *nurturance* and the need for *security*. Put a little bit more simply, we want to be nurtured and kept safe.

Being nurtured is a good thing because it means that others will give you the (positive) things you want: food, beverages, a little hugging and grooming, and perhaps financial support. Being nurtured means you will have opportunities to *gain*.

Being kept safe is a good thing because . . . well, obviously something dangerous can kill you. When others protect you, it means they will help you to avoid the (negative) things that can harm you: predators, poisons, and sharp objects, just to name a few. Being kept safe means you will be better able to *avoid loss*.

It doesn't take a psychologist or philosopher to tell you that we all want to approach pleasure and avoid pain. What's less obvious, but nonetheless true, is that there are two *kinds* of pleasure and pain, each associated with one of these basic human needs: the pleasure of being nurtured (and the pain of *not* being nurtured), and the pleasure of being safe (and the pain of *not* being safe). If you reflect for a moment on some of your own past experiences, these distinctions will become clear. The pleasure you feel when a colleague praises your work is very different from the pleasure you feel when you get into your home just before the rain comes pouring down. Both experiences are pleasurable, but they are qualitatively different (the difference between "Great!" and "Phew, that was a close one!").

What you may be less aware of is that when you are trying to seek out these different kinds of pleasure you are also sensitive to different kinds of information, use different strategies, and find different kinds of feedback motivating.

Promotion motivation is, at its core, about satisfying our need for nurturance. It's about filling your life with positives: love and admiration, but also accomplishment, advancement, and growth. Promotion goals are ones that we would *ideally* like to achieve (as in, "Ideally, I'd like to be more muscular" and "Ideally, I'd like to be in a relationship"). When we do obtain whatever positive thing we've been seeking, we feel the high-energy, *cheerfulness*-related emotions: happiness, joy, and excitement. Or, as Ray might put it, we feel "totally stoked."

Prevention motivation, on the other hand, is about satisfying our need for security. It's about doing what's necessary to maintain a satisfactory life: keeping safe, doing what's right. Prevention goals are ones that we feel we *ought* to achieve—ones we think of as duties, obligations, or responsibilities (as in, "I really need to lose some fat" and "I should be in a relationship"). When we do successfully maintain safety and security, we feel the low-energy, *quiescence*-related emotions: calm, relaxation, and relief. (They may be low energy, but that doesn't mean they don't feel good—ask any harried working mother trying to fulfill her multiple duties what she'd like most, and the number one answer is usually "to have a chance to relax.")

Before continuing, take a moment to answer the following questions. Remember to be honest—there are no right or wrong answers.

## What Motivates You?

Complete this exercise as quickly as possible. Use only a word or two for each answer.

1. Write down a quality or characteristic you *ideally* would like to possess (or possess *more* of).
2. Write down a quality or characteristic you feel you *ought* to possess (or possess *more* of).
3. Name another ideal quality.
4. Name another ought quality.
5. Name another ought quality.
6. Name another ideal quality.
7. One more ought quality.
8. One more ideal quality.

So, what do the answers tell you? If you are like most people, you had a pretty easy time coming up with the first couple of answers, but found that coming up with the third or fourth "ideal" or the third or fourth "ought" was more difficult. You can tell whether you are more promotion- or prevention-minded by taking note of *which came more easily to you*—coming up with ideals or oughts? If ideals came more quickly to you, then you are used to thinking in terms of ideals, so you are more promotion-minded. If oughts came more quickly and easily, you are more prevention-minded. If both ideals and oughts came to mind quickly and easily, then you could be high in both promotion *and* prevention. You do not necessarily have one dominant motivation. (But most people do.)

## Why a Dominant Focus?

Having just told you that human beings are wired to seek *both* nurturance and security, you are probably wondering at this point how you (and others) ended up more concerned with one or the other. The most likely answer is that it's because of how you were raised.

You might think that promotion focus is the result of having been showered with rewards (i.e., an early life of pleasant experiences), while prevention focus is the consequence of frequent punishment (i.e., an early life of painful experiences) . . . but you'd be wrong. It's actually that promotion- and prevention-minded people were rewarded and punished *differently*.[1]

Little Ray had parents who were quick to praise him for a job well done. When he brought home an A paper, he saw the pride and happiness in their faces and basked in the glow of their loving approval. He was frequently rewarded for his achievements with small gifts of toys or candy, or special privileges like staying up past bedtime. When his grades weren't so exemplary, he felt the air leave the room. His mother and father would shake their heads, sigh, look disappointed, and go about their business—leaving Ray feeling empty and alone. This is a clear example of promotion parenting, where successes are greeted with enthusiastic expressions of loving admiration, and failures are met with the *withdrawal* of affection and attention. Children like Ray who are parented this way come to see their goals as opportunities to *gain* their parents' (and later, everyone else's) loving approval. Life becomes about making progress toward fulfilling your ideals and behaving in ways that produce praiseworthy accomplishments.

Little Jon had a very different upbringing. His parents had high expectations of how he ought to behave, and failing to live up to those expectations brought swift criticism. Performing below his potential would not be tolerated. Sometimes there would be yelling, but more often he would simply be punished—extra chores, less playtime, no TV. When he brought home an A paper instead, all was well and peaceful in his household. His parents were satisfied and he could live his life undisturbed. Jon is the product of prevention parenting, where failures are criticized or penalized, and successes mean that things are okay and *nothing bad happens*. Children like Jon come to see their goals as opportunities to *avoid* their parents' (and later, everyone else's) *dis*approval and stay safe. Life becomes about meeting your duties and obligations and behaving in ways that satisfy others and maintain the peace.

Parents, of course, aren't the only influences on our pursuit of promotion and prevention goals. Temperament certainly can play a role. If from an early age you have a nervous temperament, for example, you are likely to end up prevention-minded. But even here, this is likely to happen because your nervousness made your parents interact with you differently—in ways that made you more prevention-minded.[2] So, too, can the culture in which you are raised and the environment in which you work affect how others respond to you—in ways that make you more promotion-minded or prevention-minded.

For instance, recent research suggests that Americans are, on average, more promotion-minded than East Asians.[3] Because American culture celebrates independence and emphasizes the importance of individual accomplishment, it fosters a promotion mindset. The American Dream is really a story of promotion motivation—celebrating the intrepid pioneer who reaches for the stars, takes daring risks, and goes "big." This is why we idolize innovators like Steve Jobs, self-made successes like Oprah Winfrey, and rule breakers like Erin Brockovich. (Quick—think of the last movie you saw that celebrated the life of a careful, risk-avoiding, prevention-focused person. We'll wait.) From its founding, American freedom meant the "pursuit of happiness" rather than the "pursuit of safety."

East Asian cultures, in contrast, place more emphasis on interdependence and value the groups to which we belong, like our families, over the individual. When people think of themselves and their goals in terms of their obligations and responsibilities to their group, it creates more of a prevention focus. It is about self-sacrifice and duty to others. These are the cultures that gave us Confucius, who praised family loyalty and respect for elders, self-sacrificing kamikaze pilots, and demanding Tiger Moms.

If you've ever worked on a team that you strongly identified with, you've probably noticed how interdependence can affect you. You can't afford to think only about how the outcome will affect *you*, only about your own accomplishments. You feel at least partially responsible for someone else's well-being. At times you feel a duty to self-sacrifice for the sake of the team. You don't want to make any mistakes that would hurt the team, because you know you'd feel awful if you did. You want to be someone everyone else can count on, and that is what prevention focus is all about. (And what this team example highlights is that even in America, there are times when people can become more prevention-minded than promotion-minded.)

## But Everyone Doesn't Focus the Same Way Every Time

It can be tempting, once you learn about "dominant" motivations, to oversimplify things and treat every promotion- or prevention-focused person as if they are motivated in that way *all* the time, which is, as we've pointed out, far from true.

For instance, it's not uncommon for people to have different dominant-motivations in different areas of their lives. You may be promotion-focused when it comes to your job, but more focused on avoiding trouble when it comes to your family or your finances. And even if you are cautious by nature, if your spouse has got the worry-about-everything-when-it-comes-to-the-kids thing pretty much covered, you may find yourself becoming more promotion-focused in your parenting in order to strike a better balance.

But even if you have a single dominant motivation, you will still frequently adopt the other one when the immediate situation or environment in which you find yourself calls for it. When the current situation is *unambiguously* about either gain or loss, the appropriate motivation gets triggered. We are all prevention-focused when we're waiting for the doctor to give us our test results, and promotion-focused when the winning lottery numbers are announced. (Choosing to gamble is typically promotion-focused, because it's about wanting to *gain* money, to "hit the jackpot." If you wanted to *not lose* your money, you wouldn't be playing roulette . . . you would just keep your money in the bank or under your mattress.) When your boss offers a big bonus to whoever racks up the most sales, it creates a promotion-focused environment—but when he threatens to fire the salesperson with the lowest numbers, you can feel everyone shift to prevention.

Throughout this book, when we refer to people who are promotion or prevention-focused—how they think, feel, and behave, and what influences them most—what we say applies both to those with a dominant chronic focus *and* to those whose focus is triggered by a current situation. It doesn't matter how you ended up being in a promotion or prevention focus; it only matters that, right now, that is your focus.

## What Grabs You?

When you meet your friend for an after-work get-together and he tells you all about what he did that day, or what he did while he was on vacation, you probably feel like you are paying equal attention to everything he says. You aren't. In fact, you are tuned in, whether you realize it or not, to particular kinds of information in his story—information that fits *your* motivational focus.

What kind of information is that? Well, if you are promotion-focused, the answer is: the presence or absence of *positive* events. Did he gain something, earn a reward, get a win (i.e., the *presence* of a positive)? Did he miss out on a chance to do so (i.e., the *absence* of a positive)? Promotion motivation makes us attend to these kinds of good and bad events more keenly. For example, in one study, promotion-focused participants were given a list of biographical information for a fictitious person. Later, they had significantly better memory for events from the list that were about the presence of a positive (e.g., "Since I wanted to buy something nice for my best friend, I went shopping and looked for a present") or the absence of a positive (e.g., "I've been wanting to see this movie at my local theater for a long time, so I finally went to see it after work only to find that it's not showing anymore").

The prevention-focused, on the other hand, are on the lookout for the presence or absence of *negative* events. Did he lose something, get punished, make a mistake (i.e., the *presence* of a negative)? Did he successfully avoid disaster, injury, or error; did he stay safe (i.e., the *absence* of a negative)? In that same study, prevention-focused participants were more likely to remember events that included the absence of a negative (e.g., "Since I didn't want to say anything dumb, I preferred not to say anything at all in class") or the presence of a negative (e.g., "I was stuck in the subway car for thirty-five minutes with at least fifteen passengers breathing down my neck").[4]

True story: Jon and Ray got married around the same time and took honeymoons only a few weeks apart. When promotion-focused Ray returned, he told us all about the fantastic time he'd had on his tropical getaway—the warm, blue water, the delicious local cuisine, the long walks on sandy beaches. When prevention-focused Jon was asked about his visit to beautiful coastal Italy, his first recollection was having been constantly overcharged in restaurants for bread he never ordered.

Information that fits with your focus is not only more actively attended to and remembered but, as we'll discuss in chapter 11 in greater detail, usually far more convincing. Grape juice that is described as providing positives (*more energy!*) is more appealing to those with a promotion focus, while grape juice that prevents negatives (*lowered cancer risk!*) is more appealing to the prevention-focused.[5] Similarly, shoppers with a prevention focus pay more attention to a product's reliability, while those with a promotion focus want to know about its luxury features.[6]

Your dominant focus also influences how you weigh the opinions of your fellow consumers. When you log on to Amazon to check out a product's reviews, you have some options. You can choose to go right to the five-star reviews or right to the one-star reviews, or you can read a random assortment of reviews. When you are promotion-focused (or you are looking at a promotion-focused product), a recent study suggests that you will most likely seek out positive reviews and that you will find them most persuasive. For prevention-focused buyers (and products), negative reviews are more sought after and more convincing.[7] (And if you are in the business of selling a clearly promotion- or prevention-focused product, now you know which reviews you should be concerned about.)

## Fire Photon Torpedoes!

In today's high-tech adventure movies—the kind where two forces are locked in a mortal struggle for domination or survival, and things keep blowing up with an alarming regularity—there is usually someone whose job it is to decide when to fire the photon torpedoes. (Or, if you like your action a little more old-school, substitute "medieval archer with flaming arrows" or "grizzled gunslinger with a thirst for justice" for "guy with the photon torpedoes.")

Imagine for a moment that *you* are the one given this awesome responsibility. After hours of staring at the starship's monitors (or "out at the distant horizon over the foggy moors") you see something. At least, you *think* you saw something. It was just a flash, and the equipment isn't completely reliable. You can't know for certain if it is the enemy, or something harmless like a small asteroid or some space junk, or possibly just your eyes playing tricks on you. You have a choice—fire the photon torpedo and send everyone running into battle mode, or do nothing yet and keep watching.

Consequently, there are four possible outcomes depending on the choice you make—two ways of being right, and two ways of being wrong. You could fire the torpedo and be right that it was the enemy (making you something of a hero); or you could fire it and be wrong, probably making your comrades more than a little peeved at you and wasting a perfectly good photon torpedo (they don't grow on trees, you know). You could do nothing, and judge correctly that there was no enemy; or you could do nothing and be wrong, which you'll realize instantly when your ship explodes.

Psychologists refer to these kinds of challenges as examples of *signal detection*, where the goal is to successfully distinguish the "signal" (the enemy) from the "noise." In other words, did you see the enemy or didn't you? Was it really there (the signal), or was it just space junk (the noise)? If you say "yes" and you are correct, that's called, appropriately enough, a *hit*. If you say "yes" and you are wrong, that's a *false alarm* (or, an error of *commission*). Say "no," and if you're right that's a *correct rejection*, but if you're wrong it's a *miss* (or, an error of *omission*).

If the guy with the photon torpedoes happens to be our colleague Ray, he's probably going to fire them. That's because when we pursue promotion goals, we are particularly sensitive to the potential for hits—we want to really *go for it*. And if you want to make an omelet, you have to break some eggs (and risk some eggshell in your breakfast). A promotion-focused person is willing to make an error of *commission*, but is not willing to make an error of *omission*. There is nothing promotion-minded people hate more than a miss (e.g., *not* shooting when the enemy really was there), because it means an opportunity to accomplish something was wasted. So they say "yes" in these sorts of situations. (And by that we mean situations where the right answer is unclear and you have to come down on one side or the other. So if this were a romantic comedy, you would say "yes" and marry the handsome and mysterious stranger who could turn out to be an internationally wanted cat burglar.)

The promotion-focused generally have what psychologists call a *leniency (or risky) bias*—and as a result they will end up with not only a lot more hits, but also a lot more false alarms—a lot more errors of commission. They may be a bit more likely to take down an enemy cruiser, but they are also more likely to be a bit trigger-happy and shoot at a friendly ship.

Prevention-focused people, on the other hand, are normally a cautious and careful lot, and, when uncertain, their preferred response is "no." So if Jon is manning the torpedoes, he's not going to fire a torpedo unless he is *sure* he saw the enemy, rather than risk making a mistake and looking the fool. A prevention-minded person is willing to make an error of *omission* (e.g., hesitating before firing on what turns out to be an enemy ship), but is not willing to make an error of *commission* (e.g., being responsible for firing upon a *friendly* ship). Such people really want to avoid taking a chance and having it turn out to be wrong (i.e., the false alarm). When they are currently safe, they have what psychologists call a *conservative bias*. They don't risk taking chances that could make them lose their safety. So your prevention-focused character won't marry the scoundrel-in-disguise—but this person probably won't be the film's hero or heroine, either.

It's worth noting that when prevention-focused people think they are already in danger, like when they are already being *fired upon* by the enemy cruiser, they are no longer so cautious. When disaster strikes, they will do whatever is necessary, risk *anything*, to be safe again. They are the most likely to shoot—over and over again—if they think they are in danger. But that's only in extreme cases—on a day-to-day basis, they stick to the careful, conservative approach.

These examples are meant to give you some sense of the kinds of strategies that the promotion- and prevention-focused prefer to use. Generally speaking, promotion motivation is served through the use of what we call *eager means*—ways of reaching your goal that ensure advancement or gain, and ensure against nongains by not closing off possibilities or ignoring opportunities. The promotion-focused like to make decisions by thinking about what could go right (the pros) rather than what could go wrong (the cons). Their motivation is more intense, their engagement in what they are doing is stronger, when they imagine how they will succeed—banishing all thoughts of doubt with "full speed ahead." They want to do whatever it takes to make things *go right*, even if it means doing some wrong things as well. They like to generate and consider more alternatives in order not to pass up a chance for a *hit*. If life were a football game, they'd be playing all offense—trying to win by racking up points for their side—even if it means making the occasional mistake that the other side can capitalize on. (If both sides are promotion minded, you will be treated to a high-scoring game with lots of excitement!)

Prevention motivation, on the other hand, is served best through the use of *vigilant means*. Vigilant means serve to maintain what you have by being careful and ensuring against mistakes. The prevention-focused like to make decisions by thinking seriously about what could go wrong (the cons) rather than what could go right (the pros). They are more strongly motivated and engaged when they think about how they might fail (if they weren't careful enough). Indeed, for prevention-focused people, vigilance actually *decreases* when they are confident that they will succeed. To maintain the vigilance they need, they think about what they must do to make sure *nothing goes wrong*. They like to make a realistic plan and stick to it, and avoid considering too many alternatives—seeing each alternative as a potential risk to make a mistake. If life were a football game, they'd be playing strong defense—trying to win by stopping the *other* side from scoring and by playing an error-free game so as not to lose by making stupid mistakes. (If both sides are prevention focused, look out for a low-scoring game that will be a little boring, unless you are a defense aficionado.)

## How Two Focuses Can Be Better Than One

Do you want to lose weight and keep it off? Quit smoking and never light up again? Start exercising regularly . . . and then continue to exercise regularly, for the foreseeable future? If you do, you're going to need to use *both* promotion and prevention motivation, since each is particularly suited to tackling a different phase of these common health goals.

Promotion-mindedness leads to strategic *eagerness*—really going for it with enthusiasm when you're getting started on your new endeavor. That's what you need when you begin an effort to lose weight or stop smoking—big *gains* to help you reach your goal. But eagerness is less adaptive when it comes to long-term maintenance of good health habits—what you need is *vigilance* to keep from falling off the wagon. Prevention focus, therefore, is perfectly suited for hanging on to your successes once you've accomplished them.

For example, in two studies that address smoking cessation and weight loss—those perennial New Year's resolutions—strong promotion motivation predicted higher quit rates and more weight loss in the first six months, but strong prevention motivation predicted being able to not smoke and to keep off the weight over the following year.[8]

So if you are someone who is a strong starter but finds that over time, without fully realizing it, all the gains you've made have eroded, you probably need a dose of prevention thinking. If, on the other hand, you can't seem to get yourself psyched up to tackle the challenge in the first place, a little promotion focus is just what the doctor called for. (If one or the other focus doesn't come easily to you, we'll be addressing ways to change your motivation in chapter 8.)

## Failure. It Happens.

There are times when things just don't work out for you the way you wanted them to. Maybe you didn't get the raise you were expecting. Or you can't seem to stop your late-night snacking. Perhaps you can't afford the vacation you want to take, or the date you had last Friday still hasn't called. How do setbacks affect you? How does it *feel*? The answer depends in no small part on your dominant motivation.

When people who are promotion-focused suffer a blow—when, for instance, they turn in a poor performance—it has a direct impact on their *self-esteem*. In general, promotion-focused people are concerned with having high self-esteem (i.e., a positive self-concept). Failure, as you might expect, leads them to have a more negative view of themselves and their abilities. In addition, they experience failure as an *absence* of positives—*not* winning, *not* being loved and admired, *not* gaining a reward—and consequently feel the low-energy, dejection-related emotions: sadness, depression, and discouragement.

Prevention-focused people tend to be less concerned with self-esteem and more concerned with *self-certainty*—in other words, they want to be sure that their view of themselves is correct, whether that view is positive or negative. When they turn in an (unexpectedly) poor performance, they feel like strangers to themselves—and it is the lack of confidence in their own self-knowledge that they find most disturbing.[9] (To be clear, neither promotion- nor prevention-focused people want to devalue or feel uncertain about themselves—they just differ when it comes to which they care about more.) Prevention-focused people experience failure as the *presence* of negatives—enduring a loss, being in danger, being punished—and as a result, feel the high-energy, *anxiety*-related emotions: nervousness, tension, and worry.

(Notice that when we're promotion-focused, it is when we are succeeding that our energy is high and our juices are really flowing; in other words, our engagement in what we are doing is strongest. But when we're prevention-focused, it is when things *aren't* going well that we're at our most alert and most strongly engaged. We'll return to this important difference in the next chapter.)

Now that you understand where promotion and prevention focuses come from, how they determine the information we attend to and the strategies we use to succeed, and how they make us feel, it's time to see how they influence real behavior in every area of our lives. In the next chapters, you'll see how the promotion-focused differ from the prevention-focused in the workplace and the classroom. You'll learn how they partner, how they parent, how they make decisions, and how they view their world. You name it—promotion and prevention focuses affect how you see it, feel it, and do it.

# CHAPTER 2

## Why Optimism Doesn't Work for (Defensive) Pessimists

THE WORLD LOVES AN OPTIMIST. A POSITIVE OUTLOOK IS WIDELY recommended as a cure for whatever ails you, and nowhere more so than in the United States, where a can-do attitude is viewed as *essential* to success. No surprise, then, that many self-help books touting the power of positivity are runaway bestsellers here, and that the so-called Law of Attraction—the belief that good things will "manifest" themselves in our lives if we purge our minds of "negativity"— has garnered so much attention.

It all *sounds* really good, doesn't it? After all, positive thinking is fun! What could be more pleasant than visualizing how great it will be when all your dreams come true? (And frankly, thinking about *negative* things—like the obstacles we might face or what might go wrong along the way—is just no fun at all. There's no denying it.) So being able to reach goals like being healthy, wealthy, and deeply in love by thinking only shiny, happy thoughts has a natural appeal. The Law of Attraction lets you have your cake and eat it, too! Or at least it would . . . if it worked. (It might be more accurate to say that it lets you visualize what it would be *like* to have cake to eat. The odds of obtaining actual cake this way are not in your favor.)

In fairness, there are plenty of positive thinkers out there who don't subscribe to ideas like these—they are just garden-variety optimists. *Optimism* is the belief that, generally speaking, good things will happen and bad things won't. It's often measured by assessing your responses to statements like these:[1]

*In uncertain times, I usually expect the best.*

*I always look on the bright side of things.*

*Things never work out the way I want them to.* (Optimists *don't* believe this.)

While the Law of Attraction has few fans in the scientific community, optimism itself has a far better reputation, and with good reason. Study after study shows that, compared to pessimists, optimists enjoy better physical health and recover more quickly from illness. They adjust more easily to change and are more likely to cope actively with a problem. They have more satisfying relationships and are more willing to accept a mutually beneficial compromise. Optimists are, on average, more likely to succeed in reaching their goals than pessimists, in large part because they don't give up too soon when the road gets rocky.

So optimism can indeed be a very good thing compared to pessimism. For *some* people, *some* of the time. That latter part is the part that most of the proponents of relentless positivity and optimism in the Self-Help section of your bookstore (and among the gurus of business, education, and parenting) neglect to mention—possibly because they are not aware that they are only telling half the story. As our research shows, there are those for whom the best way to ensure success is actually to believe they just might fail.

## Wait, Some People Are Motivated by Imagining How They Might *Fail*?

Yes. We realize that this may be counterintuitive. After all, it doesn't exactly sound like can-do spirit. And aren't we supposed to *banish* negative thoughts if we want to succeed?

*Not* if you are prevention-focused or are pursuing a prevention-focused goal. Because if you are, optimism not only feels wrong—it will actually *disrupt* and *dampen* your motivation. If you're sure that everything is going to work out for you, then why would you go out of your way to avoid mistakes or to plan your way around obstacles or to come up with a plan B? Seems like a waste of time and energy. If everything is going to work out, then relax and take it easy.

On the other hand, if you are prevention-focused, you can't afford to just relax and take it easy. Being optimistic takes away the vigilance you need to get the job done. Instead, avoiding mistakes and preparing for potential problems are precisely the vigilant things you feel you should do. This is, not surprisingly, something that many successful prevention-minded people have intuitively realized all along. They have silently resisted the call to positivity, understanding (perhaps unconsciously) that this sort of thinking simply won't *work* for them. Let's give you an example.

In a study we conducted with MSC colleagues Jens Förster and Lorraine Chen Idson, we gave participants a set of anagrams to work on (e.g., NELMO, which, provided you don't have to use all five letters, can be elm, one, mole, omen, lemon, melon, etc.). All were told that if they did well, they could earn more money. Then we manipulated their motivational focus: those in the promotion condition were told that they would be paid four dollars and could *earn an extra dollar* if they performed above the 70 percent level, while those in the prevention condition were told that they would be paid five dollars but could *lose a dollar* if they performed below 70 percent.

Just to be clear—everyone would get four dollars for a poor performance and five dollars for a good one, so the incentives were identical across the board. And the 70 percent level was the performance target for everyone. All that changed was how we *talked about* it (called *framing* in the psychological literature)—whether succeeding in ending up with five dollars meant you gained a dollar (promotion focus) or avoided losing a dollar (prevention focus).

Back to the experiment. About halfway through the anagram task, we gave everyone feedback. We told each person that so far, he or she was performing either above or below the target level of 70 percent. (This had nothing to do with their actual performance—we just randomly assigned them to get good news or bad news.) So they were led to believe that they were either well on their way to succeeding or possibly in danger of failing. Following that feedback, we measured both the strength of their motivation and expectations for success.

As you might expect, after hearing the positive feedback, expectations for success in the promotion-focused group soared, and so did their motivation. *I'm doing great! I'm advancing! Hooray!* they thought. Who wouldn't, right? The prevention-focused group, that's who. When they were given the good news that they were right on track, their expectations for success didn't change at all, and their motivation actually decreased. *Looks like I'm safe,* they thought. *Nothing to worry about. Might as well relax.*

What happens when news isn't so good? After negative feedback, expectations for success in the promotion-focused group went down a bit as you might expect, and so did motivation. *Hmm . . . it's not looking good. That's discouraging. Why try hard if I'm just going to end up with four bucks anyway? I might as well save my energy for something later that I can succeed on. . . .*

The prevention-focused group, on the other hand, sat up and took notice. Their expectations dropped . . . *dramatically.* These participants were quite sure they were going to fail . . . *unless* they changed things by increasing their effort. Despite that drop, or more accurately *because* of it, motivation surged! *Oh, no, I'm going to lose a dollar! Unless . . . I must do whatever is necessary to make that not happen!*

The promotion-focused really get going when they feel they are doing well. Optimism and confidence enhance their eagerness, and their motivation and performance soar. Perhaps the most defining characteristic of our promotion-minded colleague Ray is his everything's-gonna-be-all-right attitude. He takes it with him wherever he goes (including on long walks in the middle of the night through bad neighborhoods in search of great jazz), and so far it has served him very well.

The prevention-focused, on the other hand, really hop to it when things aren't going so well. The possibility of failure *enhances* their motivation, and their performance, too. Our prevention-focused colleague Jon may seem like he's torturing himself needlessly when he frets over every tiny detail of his work, but he knows that being a worrywart really works for him. (And for the record, you couldn't get Jon within a mile of a bad neighborhood even if you gave him his own SWAT team.)

To understand what works for Jon and other prevention-focused people, it is important to recognize that they are *not* pessimists in the traditional sense. They don't believe that they *will* fail or are even likely to fail. What they tell themselves is that they *might* fail if they are not careful enough or don't work hard enough. What motivates them is imagining the possibility of failure in the future from not doing what's necessary now—what the literature calls *defensive* pessimism. Pessimism—that is, expecting that you will fail—undermines everyone's motivation . . . whether you are prevention-focused or promotion-focused. Indeed, at least part of the reason why the literature has found so many good outcomes from people being optimistic is that the research compares people who are optimistic to people who are pessimistic. What is clear is that pessimism undermines motivation. Optimism, on the other hand, doesn't always enhance motivation. It does so when people have a promotion focus . . . but not when they have a prevention focus.

## Which Goals Are You Good at Reaching?

Answer the following questions using this scale:

| 1 | 2 | 3 | 4 | 5 |
|---|---|---|---|---|
| Never or Seldom | | Sometimes | | Very Often |

1. How often have you accomplished things that got you "psyched" to work even harder?
2. How often did you obey the rules and regulations that were established by your parents?
3. Do you often do well at different things you try?
4. I feel like I have made progress toward being successful in my life.
5. Growing up, did you avoid "crossing the line," avoid doing things your parents would not tolerate?
6. Not being careful enough has gotten me into trouble at times.

Your promotion success score = Q1 + Q3 + Q4
Your prevention success score = Q2 + Q5 + (6 − Q6 [reverse scored])

The questions above are from a measure developed by members of the Motivation Science Center in order to identify people with a history of success in promotion or prevention—what we call promotion and prevention *pride*. If you score high in one or the other (or both), it means that you are someone who "gets" how to work *with* your motivational focus. (It's quite possible to score high in both, since you can understand how to be effective in promotion *and* how to be effective in prevention, and this is true even if either promotion or prevention is still your dominant focus. Of course, it's also possible to score low in both. In which case reading this book may be especially useful.) To be effective in either promotion or prevention, you need to learn how to use your outlook strategically.

## The Right Attitude for the Right Job

Being effective when you are promotion-focused requires pursuing goals in an *eager* manner . . . making things happen in eager ways. Having an optimistic outlook enhances your eagerness, and thus it fits a promotion focus. In other words, optimism *works* for promotion motivation. It sustains it and strengthens it, leaving us better able to reach promotion goals. If you are reaching for the stars or taking big risks, a dose of positive thinking is just what the doctor ordered.

Being effective when you are prevention-focused, on the other hand, requires pursuing goals in a *vigilant*, careful manner . . . making things happen in vigilant ways. For successful prevention, we need to dampen or suppress our optimism, and cultivate a mild skepticism in the service of sustaining our vigilance. The maybe-it-won't-work-out attitude *works* for prevention motivation. Having a more *realistic* than optimistic outlook enhances your vigilance, and thus it fits a prevention focus. When you need to be vigilant—to fulfill your responsibilities and avoid danger—you can't allow yourself to be too confident, no matter how successful you've been in the past.

People high in promotion pride or prevention pride may both have good *reason* to be optimistic. They've both got strong track records of getting the job done. But those in the latter group know they can't *afford* to be optimistic, and they spend as little time as possible dwelling on past successes.[2] Instead, when preparing for an upcoming task—a presentation, a test, or any other challenge—they set low expectations, ignoring the evidence of their past successes. "I know I've got all A's in chemistry so far, but *this* test could be much harder—I may not do well," they think to themselves. Sometimes they even say it out loud, and get pelted with small objects by irritated classmates.

Because of their low expectations, those high in prevention pride mentally play through and rehearse all the ways in which things could go wrong—and prepare for every eventuality. As a result, they perform as well as promotion-focused optimists (and, for the record, perform far *worse* when you try to keep them from doing things their own "defensively" pessimistic way).[3]

Under the right circumstances—say, when a situation calls for careful planning and due diligence—people high in prevention pride can even *outperform* the promotion-pride optimists. One need look no further for evidence than our recent recession and the mortgage crisis that helped precipitate it. When home prices keep going up and up, people buy mortgages they can afford only if *everything* goes right (with lots of assurances from mortgage brokers that everything will). It's the prevention-focused people in an environment like this who ask, "But what if it *doesn't* go right?" and save themselves the agony of losing their home and destroying their credit.

History books and news programs are packed with examples of the perils of excessive optimism. Failures to take seriously the possibility that everything would *not* go according to plan have had profound consequences: protracted wars with staggering civilian casualties that were predicted to end quickly (Vietnam, Iraq), humanitarian crises that could have been prevented with proper planning

(Hurricane Katrina, the Fukushima nuclear disaster), and of course, economic meltdowns resulting from reckless and irresponsible investing (the subprime mortgage crisis, the Great Depression).

There is power in defensive pessimism—thinking about obstacles and the things that might go wrong (which some might disparage as "negative thinking") will give you a tangible advantage in pursuit of your prevention-focused goal. Parents who want to keep their toddler safe will benefit from scanning the home for potential dangers before anything bad happens. Adults who get regular annual health screenings are more likely to detect a problem early, dramatically increasing the odds of a full recovery. Business leaders who take their competition seriously are better able to anticipate their actions and stay ahead of the game.

One of the most important things to learn (and most difficult to accept) about the prevention-minded, whether the mind in question is your own or someone else's, is to respect their mild pessimism or skepticism and keep the pep talks to a minimum. Their pessimism is *strategic*. They know what they are doing. (And, as we noted earlier, they are not saying to themselves that they *will* fail. That could, indeed, undermine their motivation. Instead, they are imagining how they *might* fail *if* they did not dedicate themselves to doing whatever is necessary to avoid failing. Such "unless" thinking motivates them to do what needs to be done.) Only when we learn to understand and respect these two different ways of motivating ourselves can we help ourselves to be as effective as we can possibly be (and help the people we care about to be as effective as they can be).

So the next time you are tempted to give your prevention-focused friend or colleague a few words of encouragement, trying to make him more optimistic, you actually might want to reconsider. You may be doing more harm than good. (And if you're prevention-focused, then next time someone tells you to "lighten up" or says "I'm sure you'll do great," feel free to ignore her. You know what you're doing.)

## But Aren't Optimists Happier?

Sure. If by "happier" you mean that they are more cheerful and up-beat, that is. But if you mean that they have more rewarding life experiences and greater psychological well-being . . . then no, they aren't "happier." The focus in the popular media and the self-help industry (and to some extent, in psychological science itself) on "happiness" as the end-all and be-all of human existence is, frankly, far too narrow. Not everyone is upbeat and full of cheer (what psychologists call *high-positive affectives*), but that doesn't mean they aren't living fulfilling lives. This is something Martin Seligman, father of positive psychology and author of *Authentic Happiness*, has also argued in his latest book, *Flourish*.

> A mood view of happiness consigns the 50 percent of the world's population who are "low-positive affectives" to the hell of unhappiness. Even though they lack cheerfulness, this low-mood half may have more engagement and meaning in life than merry people. (p. 14)

Many of these "low-positive affectives" to whom Seligman refers are no doubt individuals with dominant prevention motivation. When prevention-focused people succeed, they may not jump up and down about it—but feeling peaceful and calm can be just as rewarding as feeling excited and happy. After all, millions of people around the world meditate to seek *serenity*, not cheerfulness. And importantly, even when prevention-focused people are not allowing themselves to feel calm and relaxed for too long, in order to restore their vigilance, they *still* experience well-being from managing to make prevention work for them.[4]

So if well-being isn't the same thing as being happy, what *does* it refer to? What is it that people want? The traditional answer among research psychologists—and dating at least as far back as Freud—has been "to approach pleasure and avoid pain." And obviously there is some truth to that. But at the same time, simply "approaching pleasure and avoiding pain" doesn't really capture what it is to have an engaged, meaningful existence. As one of us (Higgins) has argued in his recent book on motivation, *Beyond Pleasure and Pain*, what people really want is to be *effective*—to know what's real, manage what happens, and achieve the results they desire. We want to be able to interact with the world around us, and to be able to understand and manage the world in ways that allow us to reach our goals.

Why would anyone choose to endure the years of arduous training required to compete at the Olympic level, making countless personal sacrifices, if all they wanted was to maximize their pleasure and avoid pain? Why would anyone deliberately offer up their lives for the sake of their loved ones, their community, or their country, if life was all about pleasure? They wouldn't—because these aren't pleasurable choices. But they can be highly effective ones. And in the end, it's a sense of effectiveness, in whatever you do, that makes us experience life as worth living.

So promotion-focused people aren't necessarily better off than the prevention-focused, since you can experience effectiveness (or ineffectiveness) with *either* motivation. We've found that people who are high in promotion pride *or* prevention pride—people who are effective when it comes to pursuing goals because they are optimists or defensive pessimists, respectively—handle problems better than their low-pride peers by engaging in active, problem-focused coping.

In other words, when something goes wrong, both groups take action to fix the problem. And both report having fewer emotional problems (e.g., clinical depression, severe anxiety, somatization). It's clear that while optimism may be the key to well-being for some people, it's not for everyone. And given that all of us are prevention-focused some of the time, for all of us there are times when being optimistic is not the key to our feeling effective, such as when we help a two-year-old cross the street safely. For all of us, there are times to be prevention-realistic rather than promotion-optimistic.

(Note: In many studies, including some of our own, prevention-minded people do not score high on traditional measures of well-being. As we've discovered, this has a lot to do with how well-being is measured—typically, with questions that focus a lot on self-confidence and self-acceptance. Prevention motivation makes people loath to explicitly acknowledge that they are doing well for fear of lowering their vigilance. As a result, they *appear* to be less well-off than the promotion-minded. They are, however, delighted to tell you how successful they've been *in the past* or how effective they are in meeting their duties and obligations. Thus, it's all in how you ask the question.)

So if you usually are all about going forward eagerly, you should embrace optimism, and if you are more of the cautious type, you should eschew optimism for a more realistic skepticism, right? Yes. And no. Remember that everyone has both motivations—even the most promotion-focused person may shift to prevention when, for instance, a loved one becomes seriously ill. And even the prevention-focused know that vacations are times for a little more adventure and fun. To be *maximally* effective, you are going to want to match your outlook to the activity or task at hand. Most of the time, it will be to your dominant motivational focus—but not always. So remember to think of being optimistic or defensively pessimistic not as traits, but as *tools*.

To some extent, successful people do this intuitively. Psychologists call it having a *forecasting preference*—a way of looking at the future chosen strategically to maximize your performance or prepare you for what lies ahead.[5] Optimism is a good choice when you are trying to be innovative or creative or embrace risk. It's the attitude that will give you big gains. But defensive pessimism—thinking *how might things go wrong?*—is the better choice when your top priority is remaining safe and secure. And you could always try doing both together, as in the idiom "Hope for the best, but prepare for the worst."

# CHAPTER 3

## Focus on Work

Jon is usually the person who arrives at the MSC lab first in the morning, turns on all the lights, and settles himself into his (private) office. He keeps his door closed so that he can avoid being distracted by his colleagues while he works. He maintains a well-organized calendar and a daily to-do list. Ask him for a copy of a particular journal article, and he can retrieve it in about ten seconds from among the hundreds of papers neatly arranged by author in his filing cabinets. "Be sure to return it. I may need it," he says. If you forget to, he will come looking for it—because he keeps a careful log of everything he lends to his less-conscientious fellow researchers.

Ray, on the other hand, strolls merrily into work around noon. He prefers to start his day at home, reading and sometimes writing when the mood strikes him. He shares his office with three other researchers by choice, because he finds their spontaneous brainstorming sessions stimulating. Some of his best ideas have been born of these freewheeling discussions. His desk is littered with papers and Post-it Notes, including one to remind him to call his mother. If you asked him for a copy of a particular journal article, you'd better take a seat because it's going to be a while. (Which is why no one ever does ask him—they go to Jon, much to Jon's chagrin.)

Jon and Ray work very differently, and it's easy to understand why once you realize that our motivational focus determines not only our strengths and weaknesses, but also our preferred ways of managing what we do. Being able to identify and understand each focus can provide you with an invaluable tool in the workplace for increasing your employees' effectiveness, as well as your own. (Teachers and coaches take note: these findings describe what we do in the classroom and on the playing field, too.)

## The Art of Hiring

As a leader or manager, a big part of your job involves putting the right people in the right positions. But how do you *do* that, exactly? How do you assign projects and assemble teams with maximum effectiveness? You could simply rely on your intuition as to who is good at what, which may be difficult when you haven't worked with someone for long. Or you could take a more willy-nilly approach and draw names out of a hat. (As you may have already discovered, you can't really count on the former being all that more accurate than the latter. Predicting performance isn't easy.)

Or you could get "scientific" and use one of the popular personality inventories—perhaps the *most* popular one: the Myers-Briggs Type Indicator, or MBTI. (The one that tells you if you are an Extraversion-Sensing-Thinking-Judging type or an Introversion-Intuition-Feeling-Perceiving type or some other combination of its four basic dimensions.) That's got to be better than the hat, right?

Over two million people take the MBTI each year, many for the purposes of hiring, structuring teams, and identifying employees with leadership potential. There's just one small problem—*it doesn't predict performance. At all.* In other words, knowing someone is an "ESTJ" or an "INFP" tells you nothing about whether or not the person will actually be good at the kind of tasks you've assigned him or her. And in fairness to the Myers & Briggs Foundation, it does not actually claim otherwise. According to its own "Ethics for Administering" guidelines (which you can read on its website): "Indicator results [should] *never be used to label*, evaluate, or limit the respondent in any way." And from the site's page titled "Ethical Guidelines": "type *does not imply excellence, competence, or natural ability*" (emphasis original).

The irony, of course, is that this is exactly what managers need to know (and why they turn to personality inventories, which rarely predict anything useful, in the first place)—Who will be *competent, able,* even *excellent* in this position? How can I use what I know about my employees to predict their performance on a given task? And how can I use what I know about *myself* to choose a profession I will be well suited to?

One of the greatest benefits of understanding how promotion and prevention focus work is that it will give you a genuine, evidence-based window into strengths and weaknesses—the kind that translate into demonstrable differences in performance. If you are a teacher, you'll have a better sense of where a child may excel and how he or she approaches problems. If you are an employer, you'll know who should be in charge of seeking out new opportunities and who should be in charge of managing quality control. If you are a soccer coach, you'll know who should be a striker and who should be a defender. (Interestingly, professional and semiprofessional coaches may grasp this intuitively—one study conducted in Germany showed that semipro soccer and field hockey players were more likely to play in "attacker" positions than "defender" positions when their dominant focus was promotion rather than prevention.)

So, what are promotion- and prevention-focused people good at?

## Creativity and Innovation

It's hard to beat our promotion-focused colleague Ray when it comes to creativity. Most researchers work by methodically moving forward in logical increments from what is known, filling in more and more details as they go along. ("If *A* is true, then it follows that *B* should also be true, so we'll test that next.") Ray likes to turn assumptions on their head—to go where no one has gone before. ("Everyone accepts *A* as a fact," says Ray. "But what if *A* isn't *always* true?")

For instance, a few years back, Ray challenged the more or less universally accepted notion that *improving* is an unequivocally good thing. He wondered if suddenly (and unexpectedly) performing better on a task that you had failed on in the past might make you, without necessarily realizing it, a bit anxious and uncomfortable. After all, people like to think they know themselves and their abilities quite well, so surprises—even *good* surprises—can be disconcerting. It turned out Ray was right, as he was able to show in a series of clever and innovative studies. He took an intellectual risk, asked a question no one had ever asked before, and his efforts paid off.

Of course, not every creative idea of Ray's has panned out. He has sometimes spent months trying to nail down the exact experiment that would prove other outside-the-box ideas correct, only to eventually concede that he was probably on a wild-goose chase from the start. (His creative ideas *outside* work aren't always winners, either. He once had the bright idea that we go to a party and pretend to be Finnish, just to "liven things up.")

Promotion motivation—seeing your goals in terms of gain—is generally more conducive to creative thought. When people are put into a promotion focus, they find it easier to generate creative solutions to a problem. When asked, "How many uses can you think of for a brick?" they are more quickly able to go beyond the obvious (e.g., pave a sidewalk, use as a paperweight) to the out-of-the-ordinary (e.g., use it to commit burglary by breaking through windows, or to turn off your TV—assuming you don't ever want to turn it on again).

This has a lot to do with the fact that the promotion-focused are much more comfortable with taking chances, and consequently have a more exploratory information processing style. They worry less about every idea being perfect or even feasible, so they are open to more possibilities.[1] Indeed, they would be more concerned about excluding a "crazy" idea that might just possibly turn out to be brilliant. And when they do come up with something new and exciting, they run with it. Enthusiastic idea *support* is another hallmark of being promotion-focused. It's like having a built-in cheerleader.[2]

The prevention-focused, on the other hand, want ideas that are flawless and foolproof. Their critical mindset can sometimes hinder the creative process. (Interestingly, this happens at the level of the organization as well. When successful companies fail to innovate, what looks like complacency is often really a prevention-focused strategic defensiveness—a desire to *protect* the company's gains by avoiding risk.)[3]

Unfortunately, the problem with promotion motivation is that while it may be great for creative idea *generation*, it's not so well suited to creative idea *evaluation*—and this matters because, ultimately, you really do need to think critically about whether or not your idea will actually work. Prevention focus, on the other hand, leads to significantly greater accuracy when it comes to assessing idea *quality*.[4]

It's important to keep in mind that creative thinking is not the only kind of "good" thinking. Analytical thinking, the kind of thinking where people methodically and logically draw conclusions from information they are given or from what is already known, is also "good" thinking. And research by MSC Fellow Jens Förster has shown that people with a prevention focus are usually better at analytical thinking than the promotion-focused, because they stick to the information they are given and consider it thoroughly when drawing conclusions, rather than trying to "go beyond" it and complicate the problem.

So the most effective teams or organizations will solicit (and respect) input from people with both kinds of dominant motivation when it's time to innovate, while recognizing that their respective inputs will be most valuable at different stages of the process. (As we have personally found to be true with Ray and Jon. Ray is the one you take to happy hour with you after work, to come up with bold new ideas that you will scribble feverishly onto cocktail napkins. Then the next day, you bring your napkins to Jon—who tells you which ideas probably won't work, which ones can't possibly work, and which ones appear to be mustard stains. If you're lucky, he says one is "promising, but a long shot"—and that's the one you go with, because it's probably gold.)

## Paying Attention to Details

At the very end of 1998, NASA launched a much-anticipated robotic space probe called the Mars Climate Orbiter. Its mission was to collect data about the atmosphere and to act as a communications relay for the Mars Polar Lander. Nearly ten months later, it arrived at the red planet, only to disappear just as it was supposed to establish an orbit.

It had come, unintentionally, one hundred kilometers closer to the planet's surface than originally planned, which was twenty-five kilometers beneath the level at which it could properly function. Instead of orbiting Mars, it plowed right through the atmosphere (possibly disintegrating) and was lost to us forever, taking $125 million in American taxpayer dollars with it.

The problem, it was later discovered, was one of unit conversion. The team of engineers at NASA worked in metric units (the standard they had adopted in 1990). The engineers at Lockheed Martin who helped build the Orbiter and its navigation systems, on the other hand, worked in English units of measurement (pounds, inches, etc.).

When asked how an error of this magnitude could have occurred (particularly one that seemed so simple to have gotten right in the first place), Tom Gavin, chief administrator of NASA's Jet Propulsion Laboratory, said, "Something went wrong in our system processes, in checks and balances, that we should have caught this and fixed it."

This is the kind of story that makes the prevention-focused shudder, and one immediately suspects that there isn't (or at least wasn't) nearly enough prevention thinking going on in the NASA labs. It's not really surprising—these people, after all, are rocket scientists. They devote their lives to *exploring space*—if there is something more promotion-focused than that, we don't know what it is. These folks pretty much own the phrase "going where no one has gone before."

In this story there was no prevention-focused hero who averted this disaster. But it's not that there are no prevention-focused heroes in our lives. It's that they are so often unsung. You rarely get the credit you deserve for averting disaster when *it never happens*. No one says, "Way to convert those units from inches to centimeters, Bob. You just saved us $125 million and a boatload of humiliation. You rock!" Instead, the prevention-focused toil away, quietly and carefully, making sure that things work the way they are supposed to. They see to it that the airplane you are flying in won't fall apart at its seams in midflight, that the medication you are taking wasn't contaminated in the factory, and that your large skim mocha latte really *is* decaf so you won't still be up at four a.m. watching the Weather Channel.

When what you are good at is keeping things running smoothly, and things *do* run smoothly, your contribution is less likely to be noticed. So you probably won't get the praise you have in fact earned. (Unless you are the immediate successor to someone who let things go to hell in a handcart—then people will appreciate you, at least for a little while.)

Prevention-focused people are great with details—they look for them, and they remember them. (And if they think they might have trouble remembering the details, they write them down on a list. If you really *love* your personal organizer, or get excited about how your calendar and to-do list apps are fully integrated, you are probably prevention-focused.) Their vigilant approach to any task makes them quick to spot a problem, or a potential problem down the road. And because they focus on stopping losses, such as obstacles that might derail their goals, they are better at resisting temptations and distractions than those who think about their goals in terms of what they have to gain.

## Speed versus Accuracy

If Team Promotion and Team Prevention had mascots, they would undoubtedly be the Hare and the Tortoise, respectively. Like the speeding bunny who ran his fastest to win the race, promotion motivation leads to a preference for working quickly—to *eagerly* get to the finish line, and avoid missing any opportunities for gain. The prevention-focused, like the slow-moving turtle, work deliberately—steadily and carefully—to *vigilantly* guard against error.[5]

Of course, speed and accuracy are one of those classic trade-offs. The faster you go, the more likely you are to make mistakes. The more accurate you are, the longer your work is likely to take. This is why Team Promotion sometimes turns in sloppy work—they are the ones who forget to use spell-check before turning in an assignment or never seem to be able to balance their checkbooks because it takes too long to record each check. It's also why Team Prevention seems to move like molasses, checking and rechecking their work while you drum impatiently on your desk, wondering when they will *finally* be finished. (Legal departments are filled with the prevention-focused, one of the reasons why their involvement in any project with a tight deadline is met with such dread.)

Incidentally, we are certainly not saying that the tortoise *wins* against the hare, as he did in Aesop's fable. Team Prevention isn't, overall, superior to Team Promotion—any more than accuracy is necessarily better than speed. Really, it's more correct to say that for some things you want a rabbit, and for others you're better off with the turtle.

## Stability versus Change

Much to the chagrin of economists everywhere, people are not rational. But their behavior isn't random, either—it is, as Dan Ariely famously put it in his excellent book by the same name, "predictably irrational." One of the best-known kinds of predictably irrational behavior has been called the *endowment effect*—the idea that once something is in your possession, it becomes more valuable to you because it's *yours* and you don't want to lose it. (This is why, for example, people selling their homes always think they are worth more than buyers do. Also, why your spouse is so unwilling to part with the worn-out remains of a concert T-shirt from 1988—the one he insists he "might wear again someday.")

As it happens, recent research suggests that people are not always biased in this particular way. The endowment effect is most likely to happen when we engage in *prevention*-focused thinking about avoiding losses.[6] In general, prevention motivation makes us prefer stability (nonloss) over change (potential loss)—it makes us wary of switching activities or strategies in midstream. When we are promotion-focused, on the other hand, we are more willing to trade in our old stuff for new stuff, or drop what we're doing to try something else, since change represents the potential to *gain* something even better. (These are the people who will gladly exchange their current prize for whatever's behind Door Number 3. The possibility for a bigger gain is just too good to pass up.)

## Negotiation

Negotiating well is a powerful skill, but it doesn't come naturally to most people. That's because negotiation is an experience that is almost always rife with conflict. When two parties haggle over price, for instance, the buyer needs to somehow reconcile his desire to pay the lowest possible price, with the knowledge that if he bids *too* low, the negotiation may break down and the seller could walk away.

The same holds true when it comes to negotiations over salary—managers want to keep costs down, without losing their best people to better-paying jobs. And employees want to get the highest possible salary, without overplaying their hand and getting in trouble, or simply humiliated, in the process.

One key to a good outcome in any negotiation is a strong (and defensible) opening bid, since that bid will serve as the jumping-off point, as well as the frame of reference, for the negotiation that follows. You are never going to end up paying *less* than your initial offer when buying a car, or getting a *bigger* salary than you asked for when starting your new job. But a strong opening bid takes a certain amount of gutsiness—you need to overcome all those perfectly rational concerns you may have about taking things too far, only to end up embarrassing yourself and failing completely. What kind of motivation provides the necessary moxie? You guessed it—*promotion* motivation.

In one study, psychologist Adam Galinsky and his colleagues divided fifty-four MBA students into pairs and asked them to take part in a mock negotiation involving the sale of a pharmaceutical plant. Students were assigned to the roles of "seller" and "buyer," and both were given detailed information about the circumstances of the sale, including the fact that the "bargaining zone" would range from $17 million to $25 million.

Galinsky then manipulated the motivational focus of the *buyers* by asking them to think about either the negotiation behaviors and outcomes they would *"hope* to achieve" and how they could *"promote"* them, or the ones they would "seek to *avoid"* and how they could *"prevent"* them. Each pair then began their negotiation with an opening bid from the buyer.

Promotion-focused buyers opened with a bid an average of *nearly $4 million less* than prevention-focused buyers! They were willing to take the greater risk and bid aggressively low, and it paid off in a big way. In the end, promotion-focused buyers purchased the plant for an average of $21.24 million, while prevention-focused buyers paid $24.07 million. This is one of those things that's worth taking a moment to think about—two negotiators, each armed with *identical* information, facing similar opponents, and yet one pays nearly $3 million more for the same plant.

Approaching a goal with a promotion mindset helps a negotiator to stay focused on his or her (ideal) price target (also referred to as the "aspiration price" in the negotiation literature). A prevention mindset, however, leads to too much worrying about a negotiation failure or impasse, leaving the buyer more susceptible to less advantageous agreements.

## Entrepreneurship

Successful entrepreneurs need to be good at a lot of different things—they need to have bold vision, pay attention when opportunity knocks, and be willing to take a chance on their own ideas (and other people's). But they also need to avoid throwing caution to the wind—they need to assess the marketplace accurately and be able to approach their endeavor with a critical and realistic eye. So the recipe for entrepreneurial success involves hearty helpings of *both* motivations: promotion for generating ideas, taking risks, seizing opportunities, and acting quickly; prevention for evaluating ideas, tackling obstacles, and performing due diligence.[7] Entrepreneurial ventures (and, for that matter, established businesses) will likely fail when their leadership lacks the necessary motivational balance. Without promotion focus, with its ideal aspirations, your approach will be too timid to earn a big payoff. Without prevention focus, with its realistic attention to the nitty-gritty, your brilliant ideas may never see the light of day. You'll need people with both kinds of focus at the table, making decisions that cover all the bases (or that rare solo entrepreneur who is very high on both promotion and prevention).

## Who's the Boss?

Or, perhaps more accurately, who's the *better* boss? The one willing to embrace risk and innovate, or the one you can count on to run a tight—and reliable—ship? Business leaders often have unambiguously promotion- or prevention-minded philosophies when it comes to how they do their jobs. Take, for instance, these two pieces of sage advice from successful CEOs:

> *When you innovate, you've got to be prepared for everyone telling you you're nuts.*
>
> —Larry Ellison, CEO, Oracle

In other words, innovation (which we can all agree is a good thing) requires taking chances. Ellison is arguing that we need to accept risk (and ignore the naysayers)—a very much *promotion*-minded strategy for achieving success. But not everyone agrees:

> *Success breeds complacency. Complacency breeds failure. Only the paranoid survive.*
>
> —Andrew Grove, former CEO, Intel

While most prevention-minded individuals would prefer not to think of themselves as "paranoid," they would wholeheartedly agree with Grove's overall argument. Perhaps better to say, "Only the *vigilant* survive." Complacency (which we can all agree is a bad thing) is a mistake that must be avoided—a successful company doesn't get *too* cocky or comfortable with its own success. It cannot afford to relax and give its competitors a chance to catch up, and it has to imagine the competitors out there who are just waiting to take advantage of the company that fails to maintain its market position (the kind of imagining called "paranoid").

So now you may be thinking, "Hang on, they can't *both* be right, can they?" Well, the answer is yes and no. As we've argued, every organization needs the strengths of both the promotion- and the prevention-focused to succeed. But research suggests that there are circumstances under which one leadership style is more effective than the other. The key to knowing which will work best is under-standing your organization's (or industry's) operating environment—is it relatively *stable* or *dynamic*?

In a stable environment, customers have predictable preferences. You know what they want, and you are pretty sure you know what they'll want tomorrow and the next day, too. There are minimal changes in technology, and those changes are slow in coming. And you know your competition—you know precisely what you are up against. For example, the Coca-Cola Company has been operating in a relatively stable environment for decades. People want soft drinks—and they will want them for the foreseeable future. Changes in the way soft drinks are produced and distributed have been gradual. And its top competitor is still PepsiCo, as it has been for most of the last century. (Together, the two companies have captured over 70 percent of the U.S. soft drink market.)

A dynamic environment, on the other hand, is in a state of more-or-less constant flux. Customers' tastes change overnight—they are always looking for the next big thing. Competitors rise and fall so rapidly, you aren't sure who'll be left standing a year from now. Technology becomes clunky and obsolete soon after you take it out of the box. (A friend of ours has a cell phone he bought four years ago that is *just a phone*. No camera, no Web access—it simply makes and receives calls. His friends routinely marvel at it like it's a relic of our distant past, found somewhere deep in a cave with arrowheads and broken clay pots.)

If your company operates in a dynamic industry, you have to re-spond rapidly and in innovative ways to keep ahead. And as a recent study of CEOs at small firms showed, strongly promotion-focused CEOs perform especially well in periods of high dynamism. Their par-ticular strengths (e.g., acting quickly, taking chances, generating cre-ative alternatives) are essentials in an unpredictable and ever-changing climate. Not surprisingly, prevention-focused CEOs are particularly *in*effective in this kind of environment. But they are much *more* effective than promotion-focused CEOs in more stable industries, where the key to success is often avoiding catastrophic errors (New Coke, anyone?).[8]

One of the most important take-home messages from this book is that there are two *completely legitimate* ways of looking at the same goal. You may think your business needs to focus on creating new opportunities, while your colleague thinks you need to be focused on protecting your relationships with existing clients—and you are both right! Each of you may think that your approach is *more* essential, more of a top priority, than the other's—and you would both be wrong. Teams composed of both promotion- and prevention-focused people are crucial for every organization's success, but there is also the potential for infighting and poor communication.

The key is to cast aside the notion that one approach—one motivational focus—is better or more important than the other. Just as human beings need both nurturance and safety to thrive, businesses (and teams) need to excel at innovation *and* maintenance, at speed *and* accuracy. To do that, we need to respect the perspectives and contributions of both our promotion colleagues and our prevention colleagues, and to be grateful that the strengths of those with one focus can complement so effectively the strengths of those with the other focus. We can't imagine a Motivation Science Center without members like Ray *and* Jon, inspiring us to dream big without neglecting the details.

# CHAPTER 4

## Focus on Kids

*H*OW SHOULD WE RAISE OUR CHILDREN? IT'S DIFFICULT TO THINK of a question that elicits stronger opinions or more impassioned arguments. It's also hard to think of a question that generates a wider variety of answers. Co-sleeping or cry-it-out Ferberizing? Go back to work, or stay home until they reach school age? TV or no TV? Should you be a Tiger Mom (all rules and no fun) or a Self-Esteem Mom (all positive talk, all the time) or a Helicopter Mom ("Don't worry, honey, if you need me I'll be sitting just outside school in my car. You can wave to me from the window!")? Note that dads are also perfectly capable of fulfilling their version of each of these now-classic parenting roles.

The truth is, most forms of parenting have their pros and cons.[1] We can all agree that neglect, and abuse of any kind, are bad forms of parenting and should be avoided at all costs. But beyond that, knowing which parenting style is "best" for you and your child is a challenge, to say the least.

What we *do* know is that the way children are reared—the kind of guidance and feedback they receive from parents, caretakers, and teachers—has a profound impact on how they come to see the world.

So, too, does the "temperament" children have when they enter into the world, especially because it affects how others interact with them. And so it is not surprising that it is in childhood that we find the origins of whether we tend to be more promotion- or more prevention-driven.

## What Do They Know, and When Do They Know It?

Our dominant motivational focus begins to develop in infancy through our early interactions with parents and other caretakers. It continues to do so throughout our childhood and adolescence as our self-concept (how we see ourselves) and our sense of who we *want to become* begin to emerge. To understand how this happens, we need to understand how a child's intellect—specifically, the capacity to mentally represent what he or she knows—changes over time.[2]

### Infancy

By the end of the first year of life (a period psychologists characterize as *early sensorimotor development*), children are capable of mentally representing the relationship between two events, such as the relationship between their own behavior and their mother's response to it. If I cry, Mommy picks me up. If I keep crying, I get food. If I smile, Mommy smiles back. Thus, they are able to anticipate the actions of their caretaker and bring about the response they are looking for. The ability to represent this simple connection is the foundation for all the learning—about ourselves and about the world around us—that follows.

During this first stage, children experience both the two kinds of positive and the two kinds of negative psychological situations that underlie our promotion and prevention motivations:

1. *The presence of positive outcomes*, like what a child feels with a nipple between his lips, or when he anticipates seeing his mother's face when playing peek-a-boo—these experiences are associated with satisfaction and joy. This is the *promotion-focused* kind of "good."

2. *The absence of negative outcomes*, like when a mother picks up her child when he is frightened by a barking dog or irritated by a fire truck's blaring siren. These experiences make the child feel calm, secure, and reassured—the *prevention-focused* kind of "good."

3. *The absence of positive outcomes*, like when a mother stops playing peek-a-boo to answer the phone or when the child's sought-after toy cannot be found. As a result, the child feels sadness and disappointment. This is the *promotion-focused* kind of "bad."

4. *The presence of negative outcomes*, like when a child is held by an intimidating stranger or is given a vaccination, causing the child to feel distress and fear—the *prevention-focused* kind of "bad."

All infants have each of these types of experiences, though some may experience more of one kind than another. Yet two infants with identical experiences may differ in their sensitivity to these experiences. This, in essence, is what psychologists mean when they talk about "temperament." Some of us are born with greater awareness of, and responsiveness to, positive stimuli (e.g., smiles, food)—we call this *positive affectivity*. Others are born more aware of and responsive to negative stimuli (e.g., scary strangers, blaring horns), which we call *negative affectivity.* Positive and negative affectivity are highly heritable (i.e., determined by our genes) and relatively stable (though temperaments can and do change to some degree with life experience) and, importantly, make infants particularly sensitive to certain kinds of parent-child interactions.

In fact, research suggests that infants with greater positive affectivity are more likely to end up promotion-focused, because they pay more attention to and are more strongly influenced by the presence and absence of positives (e.g., when Mommy plays peek-a-boo or she stops playing to answer the phone). Similarly, high negative affectivity makes an infant really tune in to the presence or absence of negatives (e.g., when Mommy takes us to the doctor for a shot or she soothes us afterward), leading to a greater prevention-mindedness.[3]

So children's dominant motivation isn't just a product of their parents' (or other caretakers') preferred way of responding to them, because they vary in their sensitivities to different kinds of events in the world *and* these sensitivities influence how their parents interact with them. It's important to remember that babies aren't truly blank slates. Nor are they just passive recipients of whatever care parents want to give them. They come into the world with different sensitivities already in place and this can itself contribute to the upbringing they receive. Infants with high negative affectivity, for example, are more likely to induce a stronger prevention focus in their parents, who become more vigilant than they might otherwise be about avoiding negative activities that could make their child anxious.

## Toddlerhood

Somewhere between one and a half and two years of age (the *late sensorimotor and early interrelational development* period)[4] there is a dramatic shift in children's ability to represent events. They can now consider *chains* of events—not just the relationship between their own action and the response of a caretaker, but also their own response to *that* response. So they can remember that when they make a fuss or a mess at mealtime, Mommy will yell, and when Mommy yells they will feel sad or afraid.

This improvement in children's mental representational capacity introduces a major benefit for them—the ability to *self-regulate* for the purpose of creating and controlling their own outcomes. Now they can deliberately choose their actions, responses, or appearance so as to make good things happen or avoid bad ones. Because they can anticipate the personal consequences of their actions *before* taking them, children at this stage are better able to control their momentary impulses in the service of the things that really matter—the things they want most. (Sometimes the thing they want most is to pour chocolate syrup into one of your shoes or write on the wall with a Sharpie . . . *without* considering the consequences. So there are still plenty of kinks to work out.)

## Early Childhood

Between four and six years of age (the *late interrelational and early dimensional development* period) another dramatic shift in children's mental representational capacity occurs—they become able to engage in perspective taking. In other words, they become able to adopt a viewpoint other than their own. They can now infer the thoughts, expectations, motives, and intentions of others and change their own behavior to match what they believe is valued, preferred, or expected by another person.

Children are naturally motivated to learn which types of responses are preferred by the people who care for them. Although children can learn about a caretaker's preferences from his or her reactions to them personally, they can also learn by observing how the caretaker reacts to the responses of another person. For example, a child can see how his mother reacts to a brother's or sister's behavior, and infer which types of behavior their mother prefers. If my older sister Susie gets yelled at for going into Mom's purse, maybe I'll think twice before diving in myself.

This collection of knowledge—Mommy wants me to be polite, Mommy likes it when I say "thank you," Mommy gets mad when I make a mess—becomes the child's very first *self-guide*.

## The Three Self-Concepts: Actual, Ideal, and Ought

People tend to think they have a single self-concept—one coherent view of who they are that contains all that they know about themselves. But we don't actually develop one self-concept—we develop *three*. Together, these self-concepts help direct our decisions and behavior. So if you are considering going back to school to get a master's degree, your self-concepts will give you some of the information you need in order to make the decision (*Is this something my mother hopes I will do? Is this something I believe I should do?*).

The first of the three self-concepts is what we call the *actual self*—your mental representation of the attributes you actually possess right now. If you believe you are an average athlete, a below-average cook, and an above-average friend, this is the kind of information that gets stored in the actual self-concept. Next, there is the *ideal self-guide*—your representation of what the ideal version of you would look like (i.e., the hopes, wishes, and aspirations for yourself). If you (or your mother or father) dream of your becoming a star athlete, a master chef, or an amazing friend—and feel that you'll be a disappointment if you aren't—then this is what goes into your ideal self-guide. Finally, there is the *ought self-guide*—your representation of who you ought to be (i.e., the qualities or abilities that you have a duty, responsibility, or obligation to possess). So if you (or your mother or father) believe that you really should be a star athlete, a master chef, or an amazing friend—that you'll be failing your duty or obligation if you aren't—then this is what goes into your ought self-guide.

The actual self is what we usually think of when we think "self-concept," or *Who am I?* But it's the ideal or ought self-guide that answers the question *What do I want to become?* The ideal and ought selves function more like goals or standards we compare ourselves to (*Am I good enough? Do I need to do more?*). You may think you are a terrible cook, but that really doesn't matter unless "master chef" is in your ideal or ought self-guide. If it is, then you will feel bad about where you are now and will be motivated to take action to reduce the discrepancy between where you are (burning toast) and where you want to be (whipping up soufflés). In other words, you need to close the gap between your actual self and your ideal or ought self.

So if the ideal and ought self-guides represent the type of person we want to be or become, how do we decide who that type of person is? What determines the qualities that go into each self-guide? Where do our self-guides come from? Our earliest self-guides are actually mental representations of what *other people's* ideals and oughts for us are—in fact, as children, it is our parents' view of who we ideally will become or ought to become that guides our behavior. (Beginning in preadolescence, a more independent view begins to evolve—though it is still very much influenced by the views of others, including our peers.)

## The Birth of the Ideal Self-Guide

*I have placed my happiness on seeing you good and accomplished, and no distress which this world can now bring on me could equal that of your disappointing my hopes. If you love me, then strive to be good under every situation.*

—Thomas Jefferson to his eleven-year-old daughter,
Martha, 1783

Parents like President Jefferson, who tend to think about their child in terms of *how they would ideally like the child to be*—in terms of their hopes and aspirations for the child—are more likely to try to shape their child's behavior through the presence or absence of *positive* outcomes. For example, when Little Ray's behavior failed to fulfill his mother's hopes for him, she felt disappointed and dissatisfied, and would withdraw her love and attention. When parents take away something good from their child—like attention, dessert, or special opportunities for fun—the child experiences something bad: the *absence* of positives. Of course, when Little Ray was behaving in a way that was all Mommy hoped for and more, she showered him in praise and affection—the *presence* of positives.

In his book *True Compass*, Senator Edward Kennedy recalled his father's words to him when he was a boy. "You can have a serious life or a nonserious life, Teddy. I'll still love you whichever choice you make. But if you decide to have a nonserious life, I won't have much time for you. You make up your mind. There are too many children here who are doing things that are interesting for me to do much with you." Here we have another clear example of this kind of promotion-ideal parenting. If Teddy does something interesting (i.e., living up to his father's ideals for him), then he will be rewarded with attention—attention that all of Joe Sr.'s many children very much wanted. If he failed to, Father would withdraw his attention. And Teddy was fairly warned. So "ideal" parenting means strengthening ideal behavior with positives, and discouraging nonideal behavior by taking positives away.

When a child develops a *strong ideal self-guide*, it increases his or her overall promotion motivation. Thus, "ideal" parenting produces children who will be (on average) more creative, ambitious, confident, and eager to tackle new challenges.

## The Birth of the Ought Guide

*I would rather see you find a grave in this ocean you have crossed than see you an immoral profligate or graceless child.*

—Abigail Adams to her eleven-year-old son,
John Quincy, 1780

Parents like Mrs. Adams, who think of their child more in terms of *who they believe the child ought to be*—in terms of their beliefs about the child's duties and obligations—are likely to try to influence their child through the presence or absence of *negative* outcomes. When Little Jon did something that violated his mother's rules regarding how he ought to behave, he was usually criticized or punished (e.g., harsh comments, extra chores, unpleasant interventions). But when he obeyed the rules and made no mistakes, he was spared from all of it. He could go about his business in peace and at ease. So when parents take away something bad from their child—harsh comments, extra work, unpleasant interventions—the child experiences something good: the *absence* of negatives. This was Little Jon's reward for being "a good little boy." Unlike "ideal" parenting, "ought" parenting means strengthening the behaviors the child should engage in by taking negatives away, and punishing or weakening the behaviors they shouldn't engage in by bringing the negatives back.

When a child develops a *strong ought self-guide*, it increases his or her overall prevention motivation. "Ought" parenting produces children who (on average) are more analytical, better able to delay gratification and follow rules, better organized and more conscientious, and careful to avoid mistakes.

## Some Guides Are More Equal Than Others

All children end up with self-guides, but not everyone ends up with *strong* ones. This turns out to matter a great deal—a strong self-guide is both highly accessible (meaning your brain has easy access to it and consults it regularly) and particularly motivating. Weak guides, on the other hand, are easily ignored or dismissed as unimportant. ("Yeah, I have this vague idea that I'm supposed to do my homework and try hard in school, but I don't really care.") Studies show that strong self-guides come from *parental feedback* that has the following four qualities:

1. **It's frequent.** This turns out to be a very important factor when it comes to strengthening guides. Parents who spend more time responding to particular behaviors (positively or negatively), drawing attention to them, or talking about their "ideal" or "ought" expectations for their children raise children with far stronger self-guides. More often than not, one guide will be stronger than the other because parents will have a dominant parenting style. This is the style that is most consistent with their beliefs about what's important—either fulfilling aspirations or meeting obligations.

2. **It's consistent.** In general, consistency is the key to learning just about anything. If they are praised or punished for their behavior in one instance but not another, children experience

confusion about the message you are sending. Parents who disagree openly with each other, and send *different* messages to their child about what kind of behavior is desired or expected, will also wind up undermining their child's self-guide strength.

3. **It's clear.** Parents who *explicitly* communicate their rules, attitudes, and reasons for responding the way they do to the child provide the kind of clarity that strengthens self-guides. If your parents hope you will grow up to be a doctor, or believe you have a duty to be a doctor, you are more likely to "buy in" and incorporate this knowledge into your self-guide if you understand what it means to be a doctor . . . and you will understand this better if your parents explicitly tell you what would happen if you were to become a doctor.

4. **It's experienced as important or impactful.** Behaviors need to have real consequences in order for a child to really learn something meaningful about the behavior. If your children think that the positives you are offering aren't all that terrific, or that the negatives you are threatening them with aren't all that bad, then the lesson won't leave a lasting impact. Reponses that make them sit up and pay attention—because they register as important or impactful in some way—are what is needed to build strong self-guides.

In general, it is the more engaged, responsive parents who are the ones most likely to instill strong guides in their children. Parents who are uninvolved (i.e., who ignore or neglect the child or are psychologically unavailable) create weaker self-guides, because low involvement means less frequency of feedback. Children whose parents are either highly permissive (i.e., who take a tolerant, accepting attitude toward the child's impulses, make few demands, avoid enforcing rules or imposing restrictions) or overprotective (i.e., who supervise, restrict, and control every behavior of the child) are also less likely to acquire strong self-guides, because both permissive and overprotective parents respond to their child in the same way *no matter what they do.* They always underreact or overreact, respectively. When a parent's responses to a child do not discriminate among the child's behaviors, they lack clarity. How can the child know what is expected of him if the reaction is always the same to whatever he does?

We should also note that it is not just parents who are highly motivated to have their children satisfy their hopes or demands for them. Children are also highly motivated, especially when they are younger, to satisfy what their parents hope or demand for them. Take, for example, an exchange of letters between Thomas Jefferson and his daughter Martha. When Martha was a young teenager, Jefferson wrote her:

Nobody in this world can make me so happy or so miserable as you. . . . My expectations of you are high, yet not higher than you may attain. I do not doubt either your affections or your dispositions. Industry and resolution only are wanting. Be industrious, then, my dear child. Think nothing unsurmountable by resolution and application and you will be all that I wish you to be.

In her answering letter, Martha shows how eager she is to be all that her father wishes her to be:

You say your expectations of me are high, yet not higher than I can attain. Then be assured, my dear papa, that you shall be satisfied in that, as well as in anything else that lies in my power; for what I hold most precious is your satisfaction, indeed I should be miserable without it.

## Adolescence: Reinventing the Guides

Now things get *really* complicated. In the beginning, only what Mom and Dad wanted you to be or become mattered. But in adolescence, the influence of peers becomes as strong, and in some cases stronger, than the influence of parents. Many adolescents, especially younger adolescents, find it difficult to reconcile these often-conflicting demands. (Mom and Dad think I should spend all my time after school doing homework, but my friends don't think that's "cool." Who's right?) This leads to feelings of uncertainty and confusion, since the answers to the questions *Who do I hope to be?* and *Who should I be?* just got a lot more complicated because there is more than one answer depending on whom I have in mind (Mom or my best friend, Katie).

There is evidence suggesting that adolescence is often a period of uncertainty, identity confusion, and rebelliousness for children—not that living through it yourself isn't all the evidence you'd need.[5] But in particular, teens who have self-guide conflict—in the example above, the conflict between Mom's ought self-guide for me and Katie's ideal self-guide for me—are significantly more likely than those who don't to suffer chronically from indecision, identity confusion, distractibility, and rebelliousness.[6] Helping your teen identify and talk through sources of self-guide conflict, and coming up with solutions that resolve the tension—like setting aside time for homework *and* time for hanging out with friends—can make navigating this difficult time a little easier.

## What Happens When You Don't Live Up to Your Self-Guides?

The short answer is: it feels bad. Sometimes very bad indeed. Differences between your actual self (who you are now) and your ideal or ought self-guides create negative emotional states. And the stronger the guide, the stronger the negative feelings. Failing to live up to our ideal guides causes us to feel the promotion negative emotions: sadness, discouragement, and even depression. Failing to live up to our ought guides leads to the prevention negative emotions: worry, nervousness, and even severe anxiety. When the feelings are not extreme, this can end up being a good thing, because feeling bad is feedback that we are not as effective as we want to be, and this feedback motivates us to take actions that get us closer to our ideal and ought guides, which in turn will reduce or eliminate these bad feelings.

Of course, there are other ways to get rid of negative feelings besides taking action to reach your guides. First, you can alter the guide itself. In other words, you can adjust your self-guide so that your current self is actually living up to it after all. If, for instance, you ideally wanted to be a millionaire by thirty, and you are twenty-nine and your bank account balance is nowhere near seven digits, you could change your goal to "be a millionaire by forty." This is actually a perfectly reasonable and psychologically sound thing to do, since we often bite off more than we can chew when it comes to our goals. And more generally, the content of our self-guides can and should be questioned and should evolve with our learning and experience. The kind of person you thought you should be ten years ago may not be the same as it is today, and that's both natural and healthy.

The other two ways of getting rid of bad feelings are usually less adaptive in the long run. You could delude yourself about your own behavior, choosing to believe that you are living up to your guide when you really aren't. This is basically *denial*, and it is not recommended, since it is at best a short-term strategy and doesn't lead to real improvement. You could also decide to disengage from the self-guide—to belittle its importance and more or less ignore it. In this case, you are basically weakening your self-guide. And as we shall see, that's usually not a good idea.

## Are Strong Self-Guides a Good Thing?

Generally speaking, they are. Children with strong self-guides are more likely to be obedient, nonaggressive, and socially responsible. They are more likely to engage in what psychologists call *prosocial behavior*: helping, sharing, and cooperating. They have a more coherent and stable sense of who they are and what's important to them, and they can use this information to successfully navigate their social worlds. And, on top of all this, children with strong self-guides achieve more. Children with weak self-guides, on the other hand, are more likely to be disobedient, aggressive, and lacking in social responsibility and are less likely to engage in prosocial behavior, as well as achieving less.

But, to be fair, it's not that strong self-guides have *no* downside. Motivation is full of trade-offs. Since a strong self-guide can create negative emotions when we fail to live up to them, it's not surprising that they have been linked to depression and anxiety later in life. This, essentially, is the risk we take when we set strong goals for ourselves—it's always possible that we won't reach them, and we'll feel very bad about it.

But regardless of the downside, it's difficult to imagine how anyone could live an emotionally satisfying and meaningful life without striving for goals. To be effective we need to have self-guides that matter to us (including self-guides that we share with other people). So if feeling bad from time to time is the price we pay for our strong self-guides, it generally seems like it is a price worth paying. This is not to say, as we mentioned earlier, that self-guides cannot sometimes, for some people, be *too* strong and demanding. They can be. And when they are, it does make sense to reduce their strength, which is what a close friend (or therapist) can help us to do.

## Which Kind of Parent Are You?

Do *this*, don't do *that*. These words constitute the bulk of what we say to our children each day. Clean up your toys. Don't push your sister. Eat your green beans. Don't put them up your nose! Say "thank you" to Grandpa. Don't call your brother an idiot. And so on.

In the short term, we simply want our kids to do what we tell them to do—but the overarching goal is twofold. First, we want them to understand something about how the world works. Put your hand on something hot and you'll get burned. Smile at other people and they will see you as friendly and like you more. Write things down or you might forget them. The more you study, the more you learn. A big part of parenting is trying to explain the rules—that doing and not doing different behaviors have consequences, and some of those are good and others bad. . . . "If you do *A*, then *B* will happen" . . . "When you don't do *X*, then *Y* does not happen."

The second aim of all this parental instruction is to instill *values* and *goals*—ones that will make our children feel effective and be productive and respectable members of society. We want them to internalize these values and goals (i.e., adopt them as their own) so that they will help govern their behavior when they are on their own. We start by making the choices for them, but ultimately, they need to learn how to make the right and best choices for themselves.

The difference between promotion-focused (ideal) and prevention-focused (ought) parenting isn't necessarily about the kinds of values you want to give your child. Two sets of parents may seek to instill the same goals and values in their children—let's say, wanting them to do well in school, share generously with others, and be polite—but they can go about sending the message very differently. And as we've seen, it is this difference in *delivery*, rather than in *content*, that shapes a child's dominant motivation. Promotion-focused parenting delivers the message by emphasizing positives (present or absent), while prevention-focused parenting focuses on potential negatives (absent or present). Take a look at these examples, and you'll see what we mean.

## Message: It's Important to Do Well in School

### Promotion-Focused Delivery

*If you do well in school, I'll be so proud of you!*
   (positive outcome = parent's love and affection)

*If you do well in school, you'll be able to have any career you want!*
   (positive outcome = opportunities to advance)

### Prevention-Focused Delivery

*If you don't do well in school, you'll be in serious trouble.*
   (negative outcome to avoid = parent's anger and possible punishment)

*If you don't do well in school, you won't be able to find a job later.*
   (negative outcome to avoid = job insecurity)

## Message: It's Important to Be Polite

### Promotion-Focused Delivery

*If you are polite, you will always be welcome everywhere.*
   (positive outcome = social acceptance)

### Prevention-Focused Delivery

*If you are rude, no one will like you.*
(negative outcome to avoid = social rejection)

Which type of delivery sounds more like yours? Remember, all parents do a bit of both. The question is, which is more *typical* of you? If you're still not sure, answer the following questions:

### Promotion-Focused Parenting

Compared to other parents you know . . .
*Are you generous with praise?*
*Do you make a point of saying how proud you are when your child does something well?*
*Do you withdraw your attention or affection when your child misbehaves?*
*Is your child concerned with disappointing you?*
*Do you encourage your child to be confident and optimistic?*
*When you play a game with your child, do you try to let him or her win (as another way to encourage your child to be confident and optimistic)?*

### Prevention-Focused Parenting

Compared to other parents you know . . .
*Do you punish your child with extra chores (or other unpleasant tasks) when they misbehave?*
*Are you sometimes harsh or critical?*
*Is your child careful not to make you angry?*
*Are you strict?*
*Do you encourage your child to be a realist and really think things through?*

*When you play a game with your child, do you play it by the
rules even if your child could end up losing (as another way to
encourage your child to be realistic)?*

Again, many parents will see a little bit of themselves in both sets
of questions, but chances are good that one set will describe you better
than the other. This tells you something about your parenting style.

You might be wondering if your *own* dominant motivational focus
predicts your parenting style—in other words, are promotion-minded
adults more likely to adopt the promotion-focused parenting style
when they interact with their children? Interestingly, there is very
little direct research to answer this question. We do know that
promotion-minded teachers use praise more often than prevention-
minded teachers, and that the latter are more likely to use punish-
ments in the classroom than the former.[7]

It stands to reason that people who think in terms of "ideals" (or
"oughts") *in general* should become parents who think about their
children in terms of who they will "ideally" become (or "ought" to
become).

Now I (Higgins) am generally promotion-minded and I do have a
promotion-focused parenting style, including letting my child win
when we play games, whereas my wife has a more prevention-focused
parenting style, including playing games by the rules even if our child
will lose on occasion. When our daughter Kayla was ten she told me,
"Mom is smarter than you." *Well, okay,* I thought, *I'll go along with
that.* But then she said, "Mom also swims faster, runs faster, and is
stronger than you." Now, *that* I wasn't as willing to accept. I asked
Kayla why she thought that. She said, "Whenever we have a running
race or a swimming race, or we arm-wrestle, Mommy always beats
me but I always beat you!" True . . . the downside of my promotion-
focused parenting style.

We should note that although parenting styles are likely to match parents' dominant focus, there will be exceptions. Sometimes we rebel against the way we were raised by our parents. We end up feeling like we would have benefited from a little more praise, or a little more discipline, and become determined to provide those things for our own children. So your dominant motivation gives you a clue about the kind of parent you are likely to be (or might one day be), but it isn't the whole story.

## Which Parenting Style Is Better?

*Neither.* (You saw that answer coming, didn't you?) As you've seen throughout this book, promotion and prevention motivations have different strengths and weaknesses. What's "best" for you and your family has a lot to do with what you happen to value. What we *can* say, however, is that either parenting style can be awful in its extreme form.

Promotion-focused parenting is all about rewarding with love (e.g., attention, praise, affection) for good behavior, and withdrawing love to discourage bad behavior. But when love rewards are too excessive and become *spoiling*, or when love withdrawal turns into outright *neglect*, a child's self-guides will lack strength and the child will suffer for it.

### Promotion-Focused Parenting

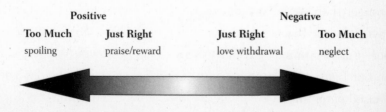

| Positive | | Negative | |
|---|---|---|---|
| **Too Much** | **Just Right** | **Just Right** | **Too Much** |
| spoiling | praise/reward | love withdrawal | neglect |

   Prevention-focused parenting is all about providing peace and security to reward good behavior, and using criticism and punishment to discourage bad behavior. But when security concerns are excessive and become *overprotection*, or when punishing escalates into *abuse*, children once again suffer from weak self-guides. They lack the knowledge, skills, and self-confidence to navigate their world successfully as adults.

### Prevention-Focused Parenting

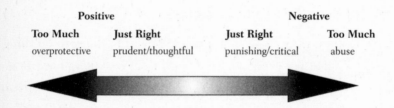

| Positive | | Negative | |
|---|---|---|---|
| **Too Much** | **Just Right** | **Just Right** | **Too Much** |
| overprotective | prudent/thoughtful | punishing/critical | abuse |

   So a sense of moderation when it comes to parenting is important. So, too, is a sense of balance between promotion and prevention parenting. It's possible for children to be both promotion- and prevention-focused, which would allow them to be effective in reaching goals using both eager and vigilant kinds of strategies. If parents give their children experience with both promotion and prevention by helping them create strong ideal *and* ought self-guides, they will have the chance to develop the skill sets to succeed in any arena.

## Working with a Child's Focus

By the time your child reaches adolescence, you will probably start noticing signs of a dominant motivational focus taking hold. (Note: Promotion-mindedness is very common among the young, but there are lots of prevention-minded teens, too.) Is she a risk taker? Does she keep a calendar and make to-do lists? Is she prone to bouts of depression, or anxiety? Does she work quickly, or take the slow-but-flawless route? Is she a sunny optimist, or a defensive pessimist?

Once you begin to see clear signs, it's important to adjust your responses to each of your children accordingly if you want to help them to be effective in reaching their goals. There are two major components to this: how they do things and how you respond.

## 1. Let them do things their way.

You don't understand why your son always wants to try to do things in a *new* way, rather than just going with what he knows has worked before. You can't see the point of your daughter writing five drafts of an English paper when the first draft seemed pretty darn good. It may not be the way you do things, but that doesn't mean it's a bad way to do it. As long as they get the results they are looking for, respect their right to choose the strategies that feel right to them.

## 2. Give them feedback with their motivation in mind.

You can throw water on a promotion-focused teen's fire if you focus *too* much on what could go wrong with his ambitious plans. You can make your prevention-focused teen frustrated and uncomfortable if you tell her to "lighten up and enjoy yourself" a little too often. It can be particularly challenging when your child's dominant motivational focus is different from your own, because what you would prefer to hear is different from what he or she *needs* to hear. Learning to speak your children's motivational language is the key—both for persuading them to adopt the right goals and for motivating them to actually

reach those goals in the face of setbacks, distractions, and other challenges. In chapters 9–13, you'll learn how to master the language of
promotion and prevention focus to both influence and inspire your
children.

## The Ups and Downs of *Good* Parenting

Tom and his wife, Rachel, have a wonderful daughter, Ashley, who is
now twelve years old. She is kind and generous to others and can tell
jokes like a stand-up comedian. She is a graceful dancer, gifted poet,
and an excellent student. Tom and Rachel have always been proud of
their daughter, whom they love very much. A few years ago Ashley
became afraid of insects, even small ones like houseflies. Her reading speed slowed down as she reread and reread each line. She
seemed to be less happy and to have less energy. One day Tom saw
Ashley pull down her coat sleeve to shield her hand (from germs)
before she opened the door to leave the apartment building. That
sight was a final blow. Something was *wrong* with Ashley. Tom and
Rachel decided to talk to Ashley about how she was feeling. They
were shocked when Ashley told them that she was unhappy most of
each day because she could not control thoughts that upset her.
Upon hearing this, Tom and Rachel each said to themselves, *What
did I do wrong?*

Tom and Rachel knew that they must have done something wrong
for their wonderful daughter to be having such problems. After all, if
they had been the perfect parents they wanted to be, Ashley would
not be suffering now.

Many parents have had the experience of their child having a
serious life problem, although the exact nature of the problem and
when it appears will differ. Regardless of what the problem is or

when it appears, parents typically react the way Tom and Rachel did. They say to themselves, *What did I do wrong?* It is not surprising that parents have this reaction. It is natural for parents to want everything good for their children. They want their children to be happy and secure, to be enthusiastic and eager to learn, to be careful and responsible, to perform well physically and intellectually, to be kind and caring, and to get along well with other people. Our culture also tells us that *all* these goals are attainable if you are a *good* parent.

Take a look at books on parenting. There are dozens and dozens of them. One thing they have in common is the message that, by following the recommendations in the book, parents can learn what to do to accomplish everything good for their children. These books, as well as experts in parenting magazines, TV programs, and so on, teach the following Standard Parenting Lesson: *Your parenting can be either beneficial or harmful to your child; children with good parenting reap the benefits and children with bad parenting suffer the costs.*

Two messages are actually implied in this Standard Parenting Lesson. First, there is a particular kind of "good parenting" that yields all the benefits for children. Second, this kind of good parenting produces *nothing but benefits*, and thus if your child begins to have a serious problem, your parenting *must not be good* in some way. We strongly disagree with this message. And by now you know why: *all* good parenting has trade-offs, because children's promotion-focused motivation (which promotion-focused parenting produces) has both benefits *and* costs, and children's prevention-focused motivation (which prevention-focused parenting produces) has both benefits *and* costs.

There is no particular kind of parenting that yields for children "all the benefits, and nothing but the benefits." Yes, there can be bad parenting, like neglectful and abusive parenting that we mentioned earlier. But there is more than one kind of good parenting, and each has costs as well as benefits. When the costs happen, children suffer and their parents suffer. But what you are seeing is the downside of good parenting and, with time and helpful intervention, the benefits will once again reappear. Don't give up on your good parenting . . . your children still need it. *Stay focused.*

# CHAPTER 5

## Focus in Love

PROMOTION-FOCUSED PEOPLE ARE FROM MARS, AND PREVENTION-focused people are from Venus. Or maybe it's the other way around. Well, whatever planet metaphor you want to use, it's clear that these two types of people approach their romantic relationships as differently as they approach everything else. Once again, it's not that they have different goals when it comes to romance. In fact, they want *exactly* the same things—commitment, intimacy, trust, and support—but they want them for different reasons. And they go about getting them using very different strategies, which, once again, has trade-offs: in relationships, there are advantages and disadvantages of being promotion-focused and of being prevention-focused. If you want to know why you have been or have not been "lucky in love," understanding the influence of your dominant motivation on your relationships is a good place to start.

## Looking at Love

When it comes to matters of the heart, we all want the same end result: to create intimacy (feelings of closeness and belonging) and avoid rejection and loneliness. But when you approach love with a promotion mindset (focused, as you usually are, on everything you have to gain), you think about the feelings of connection you hope to attain—how your love might *ideally* be. The long walks on the beach, the tender embraces, the joys that will be doubled because they are shared. Love is about new possibilities—for passion, personal growth, enrichment, and happiness. This is the version of love celebrated in films like *Under the Tuscan Sun; Eat, Pray, Love*; and anything starring Richard Gere. It's heavy on the romance, light on the realism of everyday living.

Those with a prevention mindset want love just as much, but are more likely to think of it as a source of reassurance and security—the kind that comes from feeling connected to another person and knowing you are mutually responsible for each other. They imagine how good it will feel to have someone they can truly count on in times of trouble. Love is a shoulder to lean on, a safe harbor, a strong foundation upon which to build a life together. *On Golden Pond; As Good As It Gets*; and *When Harry Met Sally* offer glimpses into this version of love—one born of comfort, trust, and trials endured together.

These two very different ways of looking at love and the role that it serves in our lives actually alter the way we think about both intimacy and rejection. The promotion-focused see intimacy as a way to *advance* their relationship, making it deeper and more meaningful. Growing closer is, in a sense, a tool for opening up opportunities for greater gains and experiencing more excitement and elation. (*The more intimate we are, the happier we both will be.*) The prevention-focused, on the other hand, see greater intimacy as a way to ensure relationship survival, strengthening the bonds that hold it together. Closeness offers us protection on the rocky road every couple must walk together, and a sense of comfort and ease. (*The more intimate we are, the more likely we are to preserve what we have.*)

Similarly, the promotion-focused want to avoid rejection because they feel that ending the relationship will rob them of the future benefits they might have enjoyed. In other words, it will cause them to miss opportunities for happiness. Rejection is a source of depression and woe. (*Think of all that could have been!*)

The prevention-focused, on the other hand, see rejection as a painful loss or betrayal. It's a severe blow to their sense of security—a feeling that one has been cast adrift, and a genuine cause for anxiety and dread. (*I feel so vulnerable alone!*) It's not surprising, then, that two people who look at love so differently would each have their own *distinct ways* of trying to get their hands on it.

## Getting Started

Don Juan. James Bond. The Fonz. Women loved them and men wanted to be like them. They were confident and charismatic and believed they were impervious to danger. Once a romantic target was in their sights, conquest was virtually ensured. Each of these famous (and admittedly, fictional) ladies' men never wanted for female companionship—though no one particular companion ever appeared to last long. For these notorious lovers, the grass soon seemed to be far greener somewhere else. Care to hazard a guess as to their dominant motivational focus?

Every relationship begins with an initial approach—one party must make his or her romantic intentions known, hoping that the feeling is mutual. This kind of risk is not an easy one to take for many of us—we know the possibility of rejection is real and that the consequences of such a rejection will be painful and embarrassing. So it's not surprising that the promotion-focused, who are natural risk takers, have a far easier time initiating relationships. The thought of a missed opportunity for romance is worse than the thought of hearing, "Go out with *you*? Seriously?"

When they meet someone they are attracted to, promotion-focused singles are also more confident than their prevention-focused peers that they are liked in return (and more optimistic that if they are not liked right now, they will be soon). This perception emboldens them, so they openly flirt a lot more. (*This beautiful woman is clearly interested in me. Better turn up the charm.*) For example, research by MSC Fellow Dan Molden and his colleagues at Northwestern University shows that promotion-focused college students pay significantly more attention to people they could potentially date, and they are more likely to actually reveal their romantic interest and attempt to initiate a relationship.[1] These are the people who eagerly try to "seal the deal."

In one particularly intriguing study, Molden looked at how dominant motivations affect the behavior of speed-daters. (If you aren't familiar with the concept, speed-dating involves meeting, for about three minutes each—hence the term "speed"—other singles who are interested in dating and starting relationships. You are seated with a potential partner at a small table in a room filled with small tables. After the three-minute bell sounds, you move on to the next person. In this way, you can meet twenty potential partners in about an hour. You rate the people you meet on a scorecard, and you are given the option of contacting those you liked best to try to set up a real date.) Molden found that, compared to the prevention-focused, promotion-focused speed-daters overtly flirted more with their speed-dating partners and pursued more of them after the night was over.[2]

Why are the promotion-minded so much more likely to initiate further contact than the prevention-minded? The short answer is: because they are quite sure that the feeling is *mutual*. As we mentioned earlier, promotion-focused daters are more confident that they are liked (and optimistic that they will be liked) by the people they themselves find attractive. Interestingly, in what can be thought of as a wonderful case of self-fulfilling prophecy, they are correct. Thanks to a process psychologists call *reciprocal attraction*, it turns out that as a rule we are more attracted to people who send signals that they are attracted to us. Even in as little time as three minutes, promotion-focused speed-daters are able to convey their interest in their partner, and are in turn rated as more attractive by their partner.

It's worth pointing out at this point that the promotion-focused don't have lower standards about who is worthy of their romantic attention. So it's not that they are casting a wider net—it's that they are actually *casting* their net. The prevention-focused find just as many potential partners attractive, but are less likely to show interest or to try to initiate a relationship. The risk of rejection looms larger for them, so their love is more likely to go unrequited. Shakespeare once wrote, "If thou remember'st not the slightest folly that ever love did make thee run into, thou hast not loved." Well, the prevention-focused are particularly uncomfortable when it comes to "folly." They are more likely to want to play it safe and protect themselves from making an embarrassing and painful mistake, and as a result, they have a harder time getting things started.

Our colleague Jon's approach to romance has always been as prevention-focused as his approach to his work. During his first years as a graduate student, he was single. Almost stubbornly so. The frequent attempts the MSCers made to take him out to meet a nice girl were consistently rejected. He wanted no part of the singles scene, confident that he would not be successful in that environment. Truthfully, he was probably right—pleasant small talk was never his strong suit. Eventually, he was introduced to someone through a family friend (against his will), and they hit it off. If by "hit it off" you mean that they each thought the other one lacked the kinds of flaws that would be a deal breaker. They dated for several years before getting engaged, and then waited several more to get married, just to be on the safe side.

Ray, on the other hand, was what some might call a serial monogamist. He seemed always to be falling in love, but his partner changed about as often as he remembered to do his laundry—which is to say, every couple of months. Between girlfriends, he was a regular at singles nights, where his easy charm made him popular despite the deficiencies in his wardrobe. Now happily married to his "soul mate," Ray continues to gush about how being with his wife has helped him to mature and develop as a person. (His wife, who, interestingly, is much more prevention-focused, rolls her eyes at this and reminds him to pick up the dry cleaning on the way home from work.)

Incidentally, there is another interesting difference in how the promotion- and prevention-focused strategically approach romance—specifically, how they try to make a good impression on potential partners. Both types engage in what psychologists call *impression management*. Basically, this means you try to present yourself in the best possible light. (Or as some have called it, "hide the crazy.") For the prevention-focused, it's fairly deliberate and strategic—they know they're not showing you everything there is to see, and they also know that they are not as wonderful as they are coming across. The promotion-focused also put on a good show, but the difference is, they actually buy into their own hype. In their eyes, they are genuinely every bit as awesome as they would have you believe. We call this *self-deceptive enhancement*, to reflect the fact that it's less about fooling you and more about fooling themselves.

## Moving Ahead

Let's say you've made it to the first date. The first major obstacle to romance has been overcome. But now you have to ask yourself, *Will there be a second? Is this the start of something big?* Getting from the first date to "we're in a committed relationship" isn't easy. But the more two people trust each other, give each other their attention, and disclose personal and intimate details about themselves (e.g., their dreams, their deepest fears, their obsession with *Star Wars*), the more likely a relationship will really get going.[3]

Here, promotion-minded people once again seem to have the advantage. They are quicker to trust and, consequently, reveal personal details to their partner. This, in turn, heightens intimacy and mutual commitment, which moves the relationship nicely along. They are also more trusting than the prevention-minded are in the wake of a betrayal—for instance, when they catch their partner in a lie—and are able to return more quickly to prebetrayal levels of trust if the injury is not repeated.[4]

Now, in fairness to the prevention-minded, being quick to trust is not always such a good thing. (We're sure that some of the prevention-minded readers of the previous paragraph were thinking, "Sounds like a sucker to me," and undoubtedly that's sometimes the case.) And you could argue that trusting in the wake of a betrayal is particularly unwise, since a betrayal is evidence that your partner is not in fact trust*worthy*. It is therefore perhaps better to say that, rather than having an advantage in the early stages of a budding relationship, the promotion-minded have a different strategy: err on the side of trust. The prevention-minded, instead, err on the side of caution—and their relationships develop more slowly, when they develop at all.

## The Language of Romance

Are we boyfriend-girlfriend, or just friends? Friends with benefits? Dating? Seeing each other? Exclusive or open? Looking to get married, or looking to have fun? There are countless ways for couples to define the parameters of their relationship, if they so choose. But not everyone feels the need to "label" their current state of affairs. And by "not everyone," we mean "promotion-focused people" who are open to different possible options and the different labels that go with them. Prevention-focused people, on the other hand, *hate* having a lack of clarity in their relationships. They want to know exactly where they stand, what the rules of the relationship are, and if everyone is playing by them. In fact, research suggests that if there is one thing the prevention-focused are more uncomfortable with in relationships than blind trust, it's ambiguity.[5]

Unfortunately, it's quite difficult to have a relationship, particularly in its beginning stages, without *some* ambiguity. If you just can't tolerate it, then you have to resolve that ambiguity, using one of three options. Option one is to have the "Where do you see this relationship going?" conversation. This is technically referred to as "the Talk." Because it is so difficult to initiate the Talk without sounding needy or clingy, people preparing for it will often spend hours in advance conferring with friends, to develop an approach that captures the perfect balance of casualness and interest. Good in theory, but very difficult to do in practice—which is why the Talk is put off for as long as the prevention-focused person can stand to put it off before the ambiguity drives him or her crazy.

Option two for dealing with ambiguity is to, as Sting once put it, "build a fortress around your heart." Put up walls, create excuses for leaving the relationship where none exist, and reject *the other person* before he or she rejects you. Everyone knows someone who approaches their relationships this way—love saboteurs who gum up the works intentionally so they won't have to make themselves truly vulnerable. While this *is* one way to get rid of ambiguity, it's also a great example of failing to give love a chance.

Option three for dealing with ambiguity is when people *test* whether their romantic partner *really* loves them. They become very demanding, impossible to live with, and they check whether their partner responds to their every wish and forgives their every transgression. Again, this might reduce ambiguity but it is a classic case of *self-fulfilling prophecy*, where people act on their anxious belief that they are not truly loved, which, over time, destroys their partner's love for them.[6]

## What Kind of Fool Am I?

Relationships are a two-way street. There is give, and take, and then give again. Attraction, interest, and trust are all reciprocal in nature—they need to be returned in order to grow, or to even be sustained. So your relationship satisfaction isn't only about how much you like your partner; it's also about how much he or she seems to like you back. It isn't just about how much you bare your soul, but also about how responsive your partner is to the soul baring.

Whenever it takes more than one person to make something work, there is a decent chance that it will be sabotaged by misperception and miscommunication. There are so many ways to misread each other's intentions. You can see attraction and interest where none exist, or fail to even recognize them when you see them. It can be difficult to know when to take no for an answer, or, on the other hand, you can see full-blown rejection in even the slightest criticism. Love makes fools of us all—but your dominant motivation tells you a lot about the *kind* of fool you are likely to be.

The promotion-focused fool in love is the *overeager fool*. These people are particularly sensitive to positives (e.g., a loving glance, an anniversary remembered) and relatively *in*sensitive to negatives (e.g., how lately she's been spending a lot more time with her "friend"

Steven). So they are likely to pay selective attention to positive signals and are also more likely to interpret an ambiguous signal in a positive way. Much like Pepé Le Pew, the amorous skunk from Looney Tunes who was blissfully ignorant that his "amour" was absolutely not interested in him, they may continue their passionate pursuit long past the point at which it is welcome.

Far from being too eager, prevention-focused partners tend to be *hypervigilant fools*. They are prone to accentuating the negative (and will be all too aware of how much time she is spending with Steven). Unfortunately, they are sometimes so preoccupied with avoiding rejection that they end up seeing rejection where it doesn't necessarily exist.

Knowing what kind of fool you are likely to be can help you to avoid derailing a relationship that might otherwise have succeeded. If you are promotion-focused, know that you may have a tendency to come on too strong and to assume that you are both on the same page when the signs clearly indicate that you are not. You may need to learn to take it slow. If you are prevention-focused, know that you are probably a bit overly sensitive to rejection. You may react defensively when you aren't really under attack. You might need to learn not to jump to the worst conclusion.

## When Things Go Wrong

Even when misperception and miscommunication are not sabotaging a relationship, every couple eventually runs into bumps in the road. And the way you handle conflicts has a lot to do with your dominant motivation. During arguments and disagreements, prevention-focused people tend to see their partners as more intentionally distant, and less supportive of their own wants and needs. Being detail oriented by nature, they approach their relationship troubles the same way—focusing on the details of the conflict itself, rather than on the "big picture" of the relationship as a whole. As a result, they experience more worry and agitation. (If you are wondering if you are prevention-focused in your relationship, answer the following question: Has your partner asked you, on more than one occasion, why you can't just *let it go*? If yes, that's a pretty sure sign.)

Promotion-focused people, on the other hand, perceive their partners as more supportive; use more creative solutions to address conflict; and experience more sadness and discouragement, rather than agitation, when things go wrong.[7] But lest you think their more positive attitude in an argument lets them off the hook entirely, remember that their inattention to detail also makes them the ones who are more likely to behave irresponsibly, act impulsively, and forget your anniversary. So odds are good that when it comes to conflicts from one partner not behaving as he or she should have, it's the promotion-focused partner whose misbehavior started it.

## Should I Stay or Go?

People are pretty predictable when it comes to their investments. You hand your money over to a banker or broker under the assumption that it will yield benefits. You are more reluctant to pull your money back out of the investment if there are large penalties—in other words, money that you won't get back. But you will be more willing to do so if another fantastic investment opportunity with an even greater yield presents itself.

Relationships, it turns out, are more like investments than we might like to think. We want a fair return on our investment. You put in your resources (in this case, time, effort, and attention instead of money; though sometimes, there's money involved as well). And then you get something in return for your investment—something that makes it all worthwhile for you.[8] Psychologists who study relationship commitment find that, much as you would handle any investment, you are more likely to stay committed to your partner if (1) you are satisfied that the benefits do in fact outweigh the costs, (2) you have already invested resources into it that you can't get back out (i.e., the *sunk costs*), and (3) there aren't any particularly good alternative partners in view.

So when your satisfaction is reasonably high, your sunk costs are significant (say, because you have spent years with this partner building a life together), and the grass doesn't seem greener with someone else, your commitment to your current relationship tends to be strong. A large enough shift in any one of these factors (e.g., your partner is making you miserable, you haven't been together long, your very attractive new coworker is flirting with you) can spell relationship trouble.

Promotion- and prevention-focused people tend to be equally committed to their relationships, but they aren't influenced to the same degree by each of these three factors that contribute to commitment. Prevention-focused partners focus less on the relationship benefits and more on sunk costs—they hate the idea that they will lose everything they have worked so hard to build and be left with nothing to show for it. Also, they are motivated to maintain a satisfactory relationship rather than switch when they think another relationship could be even better (i.e., an advancement) . . . indeed, their natural skepticism makes them unlikely to think that another partner would be any better than the one they currently have. They tend to prefer the devil they know to the one they don't—even if the devil in question turns out to be their spouse. If you (or someone you know) have "stuck it out" in an unhappy relationship *while telling yourself that it's not so bad . . . things could be worse*, then you (or that other person) are probably prevention-focused.

Promotion-focused partners, on the other hand, think that the grass just might indeed be greener somewhere else, and they are far less sensitive to a relationship's sunk costs. You would think that this would make them abandon relationships sooner, but they don't— because satisfaction is what matters to them, and they have a *positivity bias*. Remember that the promotion-focused pay particular attention to, and have better memory for, positive outcomes and experiences. They are also optimists by nature—the kind that thinks things like "He can change (for the better), I just know he can!" So they tend to see their partners and interpret their actions in the best possible light, which helps them to sustain their commitment even while dating a selfish jerk. If you (or someone you know) keep trying to make an unhappy relationship work *while telling yourself that things are sure to improve*, then you (or that other person) are probably promotion-focused.

## Forgive Me

Everybody makes mistakes. No one is perfect. So in order for relationships to last, a little forgiveness is needed now and again. Of course, whether or not you forgive your partner's transgression depends a lot on its magnitude—did he cheat on his heart-healthy diet, on his taxes, or on *you* with his secretary? Your forgiveness also depends on your dominant motivation, in a couple of interesting ways.

First, promotion- and prevention-focused people forgive for different reasons. Promotion-focused people forgive for the possibility of future gain, and they do so as a function of trust. In other words, the more they trust you, the more likely they are to forgive you so you can continue to reap the benefits of the relationship.

Prevention-focused people forgive in order to avoid further loss, and they do it as a function of commitment. So the more committed they are to the relationship itself, the more likely they are to forgive you in order to preserve it.[9]

In addition, apologies can be significantly more effective, and more likely to lead to forgiveness, when they are expressed in a way that matches the injured party's motivation.[10] How does that work, exactly? Read the examples below—the key words that shift the apology's focus are highlighted.

### Promotion-Focused Apology

I'm so sorry and I have to apologize for what happened. *I am hopeful that our relationship can move forward after this.* I feel terrible and I want you to know that *I will strive to do whatever it takes to gain back your trust.*

### Prevention-Focused Apology

I'm so sorry and I have to apologize for what happened. *I am responsible for this and I feel it's my duty to repair our relationship.* I feel terrible and I want you to know that *I feel obligated to do whatever it takes to not lose your trust.*

As we'll see in the chapters that follow, matching your language to your listener's dominant motivation is a great way to convey a message that *feels right* and is more persuasive to the listener. And that's as true for relationships as it is for marketing products.

## Which Couples Are the Best Couples?

We realize that by even asking that question, we're heading into dangerous territory. But you can tell a lot about how two people will relate to each other by knowing their dominant motivations, as some pairings work very differently than others.

## Promotion-Promotion Couples: The Whirlwind Romance

These are the people who take the fast train to romance. We don't know if fools actually rush in, but the promotion-focused couple is likely to. Commitment and intimacy skyrocket as each lover trusts and discloses, and then trusts and discloses in return. Giddy with eagerness, their new love is all sunshine and roses. Until, of course, it isn't—but that comes later.

These are the kinds of romances many of us can remember having when we were younger—when the boy or girl you fell for at fifteen was clearly your One True Love. As was the one you fell for at sixteen, and then again the one at seventeen, and so on. The protagonists in tales of star-crossed lovers are also usually promotion-focused. If Romeo and Juliet had been prevention-minded, they would have been much more sensitive to the troubles their love would bring, and not nearly so foolish as to attempt to fake their own deaths—how many ways can *that* go wrong? The writers of most love songs are promotion-focused, too. *You and I will make each night a first, every day a beginning . . .* sounds a lot more romantic than *You and I will make each night more comfortable, every day safer. . . .*

There are, indeed, many ways in which having a promotion-focused partner can benefit you. Research shows that such people are more likely to try to help move you toward becoming your ideal self—to be all that you can be. They do this through a process that includes frequent affirmation (*You are the greatest!*), providing opportunities for self-development (*You've always wanted to try yoga, so I brought you home a brochure from the studio around the corner*), direct assistance (*Do you want my help with your resume?*), and challenging (*How can you settle for this job when your great talent would be wasted?*).[11] Psychologists refer to this kind of relationship support as the *Michelangelo phenomenon*, because like the artist, your partner "releases the sculpture from the marble," helping you to reach your fullest potential.

Of course, as wonderful as that sounds, there are plenty of times when the recipient of all this sculpting doesn't appreciate the effort. She may feel that her sculpture is just fine, thank you very much, *without* any more chiseling. It's also true that the sculpture inside may not be what the partner imagines it to be. Give an optimist a lemon, and he makes lemonade—but trying too hard to make lemonade from your relationship lemon can cause a lot of tension, hurt, and frustration.

### Prevention-Prevention Couples: The Slow and Steady Romance

If promotion-promotion romances are like a fast train, prevention-prevention romances are like a wagon train—inching their way along and stopping frequently to rest the horses. Intimacy is achieved in small, slow, and steady increases as a deepening sense of trust gradually emerges. It's the kind of love story Jane Austen so often wrote about, where two would-be lovers who dare not reveal their true feelings take *the entire book* to finally work up the courage to say something like, "I hold you in the highest personal regard, Miss Bennet."

But even if they are slow to warm up, prevention-focused partners are particularly devoted once they do. Research suggests that they are, for instance, more willing to merge their own goals with their partner's. They are also more likely to adapt to their partner's goals, career, and priorities and try to accommodate their partner's needs. Promotion-focused partners may be more likely to praise each other's accomplishments, but prevention-focused partners are more likely to sacrifice their own needs to make their loved one's accomplishments possible.[12]

Jon and his wife are an excellent example of prevention-focused mutual devotion. Jobs in academia are scarce relative to the number of people seeking them, so young researchers are often forced to take positions in far-flung satellite campuses of universities, hundreds of miles from family and friends. Jon's wife has willingly made such sacrifices in order to follow Jon to places she'd never dreamed of living, solely in order to support his career. Similarly, we rarely see Jon at annual conferences (and we psychologists *love* our annual conferences), because he is reluctant to leave his wife with the burden of caring for their young children alone for days at a time. Neither of them gush publicly about the other, and we doubt very much that they bother with things like "date nights." But they show their love for each other in countless ways, through the selfless support they are both so willing to give.

## Promotion-Prevention Couples: Divide and Conquer

On the face of it, promotion-prevention pairings should be a disaster. There's nothing like having two completely different ways of looking at basically everything when it comes to setting the stage for conflict. He embraces risk; she avoids it. He is an optimist; she is a (defensive) pessimist. He is spontaneous; she lives by her daily planner. He speeds; she's quick to put on the brakes to make sure they are heading in the right direction. We all know how well two peas in a pod get along—but what happens when it's a pea and a potato?

Oddly enough, the best relationships (and by "best," we mean something like "most adaptive and mutually satisfying") may in fact be the Odd Couples—duos with a mix of dominant promotion and prevention focus. As we saw from the workplace examples in chapter 3, there are clear advantages to being able to "divide and conquer" your various pursuits—and that's true in your personal life, too. In a mixed-motivation couple, you don't have to be the person who makes *everything* happen. Each person can take on the tasks he or she is best suited for, knowing that the partner has got the other stuff covered. (He can come up with the plan for a great vacation; she can make sure they actually get there with everything they need.) This is particularly true for married couples, who usually have goals related to both advancement and security. They need to help each other in order to both reach their dreams *and* fulfill their responsibilities.[13]

Not surprisingly, then, recent research shows that mixed-motivation married couples do indeed have greater relationship satisfaction than all-promotion or all-prevention pairings. But there is one very important caveat—the couple in question must have *shared goals*. In other words, both partners need to see their goals as a joint effort, as shared goals that benefit from a division of labor in reaching them.[14] They need to feel that they are on the same page in terms of what they want, and differ only in terms of their preferred ways of getting it, with the promotion-focused partner being given the eager parts of the joint task (e.g., creating a new sauce for the dish they are preparing together) and the prevention-focused partner being given the vigilant parts (e.g., checking the time and temperature during cooking). When goals are shared, everybody gets to do things the way they like to do them, without fighting over whose approach is the right one. All that can be a recipe for lasting love.

Writing this, we realize that we are both in mixed-motivation marriages that have these potential benefits. It can make for good teamwork and help to reduce *over*eagerness (a potential downside for promotion-promotion couples) and *hyper*vigilance (a potential downside for prevention-prevention couples). But, as we mentioned earlier, the secret is to have shared goals, and this is not always easy to achieve. And until it is, there can be focus-driven arguments:

That investment is too risky.
> But that's how you make money!

You let our daughter do *what?*
> You never let her be adventurous!

Let's go somewhere new for vacation this year.
> We love the cabin—why mess with a good thing?

With mixed-motivation couples, family life has the potential to be more balanced—children know how to be optimistic *and* realistic—because the partnership contains both the promotion and prevention points of view. And the marriage partners have someone in their lives to remind them that life isn't all about gains *or* isn't all about avoiding losses. On the other hand . . . and there is always another hand . . . the promotion-promotion couples and the prevention-prevention couples, where the marriage partners have similar perspectives, more naturally achieve shared goals and have shared preferences for how to attain them. This reduces the likelihood of conflicts. As always, there are trade-offs.

# CHAPTER 6

## Focus on Making Decisions

THROUGHOUT YOUR DAY, YOU PROBABLY SPEND MORE TIME MAKING decisions than you do anything else, other than breathing. Many of these decisions are largely unconscious—hitting the brakes when the car in front of you slows down is a decision, though because it happens quickly and without conscious thought, it may not feel like one. But when we *are* consciously aware that we are making a deliberate decision—whether it's to see a movie, go on a blind date, or get a flu shot—we generally do so by weighing the pros and cons. Which looks something like this:

*The previews for this movie look terrific, but paying for the ticket, some popcorn, and a drink may force me to take out a second mortgage.*

*Sarah says he's a really great guy, but blind dates are so awkward and uncomfortable.*

*It's good to be protected from the flu, but I really hate needles.*

Most of us like to think that we are pretty good at weighing the pros and cons in an even, unbiased way. And that after doing so, we come to a rational, objective conclusion—the same one that any other reasonable person would come to. But when we think that, we are wrong—because we do nothing of the sort. Instead, we favor certain kinds of information over others and make decisions loaded with biases. *Which* information gets favored, and *which* biases sway our thinking, depends a great deal on our motivational focus.

Promotion-focused people usually make decisions by emphasizing the answer to the following question: Why would doing X be a *good* idea, and what will I miss out on if I don't do X? *Why would it be good to see this movie, and how good would it be? Why would this blind date be worth going on? Why is it good to get a vaccine?* If the answer is fairly compelling, then they go for it. If it doesn't seem all that great, they don't bother. And they feel right about making decisions this way, because they have thoroughly considered the potential positives.

Prevention-focused people, on the other hand, usually make decisions by emphasizing the answer to a different question: Why would doing X be a *bad* idea, and what kind of trouble could I aviod if I don't do it? *How much will seeing this movie cost? How uncomfortable am I likely to feel on this date? How painful will the shot be?* If the answer is not particularly alarming, then they go for it. If it *is* alarming, then forget it. And this feels like the right way to make a decision for a prevention-focused person, because it involves taking the potential negatives seriously.

So promotion-focused people think more about the pros when making decisions, and prevention-focused people are more interested in the cons. Doesn't sound totally rational and objective, does it? (This doesn't mean, incidentally, that they'll always come to different conclusions—after all, the choice with the most pros is sometimes the one with the least cons, too.) Giving more weight to positives or to negatives is just one of the many biases that our dominant motivation creates.

## More Than One Way to Skin a Cat?

How do you usually solve problems? Suppose we ask you to take a large sum of money—say, $100,000—and present us with your recommendations for how to invest it. You spend a week or so doing some research on investments and put together a brief report. If you are promotion-focused, your report will almost certainly include several options for us to choose from, because the promotion-focused love to generate *alternative solutions* for problems. Precious metals look good, but so does the technology sector. Then again, American auto stock is performing well. Or you could go with something a little more high risk–high reward, like a start-up. Why narrow it down to just one recommendation, they think, when each solution is a potential winner—another opportunity to *gain*. Why limit yourself? (If you walk into a restaurant and there are one hundred different burgers on the menu—which actually does happen—it's likely that the chef is promotion-focused.)

If, however, you are more prevention-focused, then your report will probably offer a single (conservative) recommendation (*How about an annuity?*). Prevention-focused people don't like many options—they find a solution that they think will do the job and then they stick with it. To them, each new (and unnecessary) solution creates new potential for error—another way to make a mistake. Better to just find the one best solution (through careful analysis and deliberation, of course) and get on with it. (If you walk into a restaurant and there is *no* menu—you just get whatever the chef has decided to make that day—then he is probably prevention-focused.)

Our colleagues Jon and Ray use these same strategies when it comes to how they conduct research. Prevention-focused Jon—despite having a very broad knowledge of motivation in particular and psychology in general—has spent the last decade studying a single, albeit central, motivational issue in extraordinary depth. (We would tell you which one, but then you might know who he is. And then we might be in hot water.) Rather than risk spreading himself too thin, he has decided to thoroughly master one domain of knowledge.

Promotion-focused Ray, on the other hand, has always preferred to have a lot of pots on the stove. He has published motivational studies in areas as diverse as achievement, group dynamics, stereotyping, aging, and social information processing. (There are probably more that we are forgetting.) Why focus on one issue, Ray thinks, when there are so many interesting questions that need answering?

Notice that these are essentially the same attitudes both men took toward dating during their bachelor days. Find one good partner and date that person forever, since every other potential partner might be a disaster (Jon's strategy), or try out *lots* of different partners, since each one might be better than the last (Ray's strategy).

## Find the Right Level

Imagine that you are interested in buying an elliptical trainer (ignoring for the moment the fact that you already own a stationary bike that you mostly use as a place to hang wet towels). Read the two descriptions of the fictional Samsa elliptical trainer below:

### Samsa: The Ultimate Aerobic Machine for a Great Workout!

Why exercise with the Samsa Elliptical Trainer? Because it gives your body complete conditioning while you achieve cardio-vascular training, and ensures that you get buff!

or

## Samsa: The Ultimate Aerobic Machine with the Right Features!

How can you exercise with the Samsa Elliptical Trainer? Its no-impact stepper is designed to cushion each step, while the multiple incline setting complements the precise, patented geometry of your stride.

What's different about them? Not sure? How about these two ads for a fictional new flash drive, the Melody:

### Melody Flash Drives

Having your data in your pocket is music to your ears!

or

### Melody Flash Drives

Get 2-in-1: a data storage device and an MP3 player!

If you guessed "one seems more abstract, while the other is more concrete," you are correct. Just about anything can be described, and then represented in your mind, in relatively abstract or concrete terms. Psychologists call this *construal level*. High-level (abstract) construals focus on the *why* of an activity—what's desirable about doing it. In the first Samsa and Melody ads, you're being told why you should buy this particular piece of equipment—the purpose it serves. We like to call this "Big Picture" thinking.

Low-level (concrete) construals focus on the *how* of an activity—whether or not you can actually do it, and the steps you'll have to take. In other words, they focus on *feasibility*, rather than desirability. Is this possible? Will it succeed? The second Samsa and Melody ads were designed to emphasize how you would use the equipment—the actual mechanics of what it is and how it works. This kind of thinking is more about the "Nitty-Gritty," rather than the Big Picture.

Because promotion-focused people are sensitive to the potential for gains, they are more likely to think Big Picture. They want to know *why* the product or action is desirable—that's what they're looking for in its description. The prevention-focused, on the other hand, want to be safe and think things through, so are more likely to think Nitty-Gritty. They want to know about the feasibility of using this product or taking this action—*how* does it work, and will it work reliably?[1]

Emphasizing the Big Picture (*why*) or the Nitty-Gritty (*how*) has been shown not only to influence how appealing a particular product is for promotion- and prevention-focused consumers, but also to more effectively motivate them to *do* things, like exercise.[2] For example, arguing, "Exercise helps you maintain a healthy weight!" is more effective for motivating promotion-minded people, because the message is all about why you exercise. On the other hand, "Exercise burns over 400 calories an hour!" is more motivating for prevention-minded people, because the message focuses on how exercise works.

So understanding whether you need to empasize the *why* or the *how* when lighting a fire under your audience is essential, and in the real world we get it wrong sometimes. In 2009, the much-beloved children's program *Reading Rainbow* came to an end because it lost its funding. The show, starring LeVar Burton, was focused on instilling in kids a lifetime love of reading. It aired for twenty-six years (longer than any other children's series in PBS history, save *Sesame Street* and *Mr. Rogers' Neighborhood*). Here's why it ended:

> [Station content manager John] Grant says the funding crunch
> is partially to blame, but the decision to end *Reading Rainbow*

can also be traced to a shift in the philosophy of educational television programming. The change started with the Department of Education under the Bush administration, he explains, which wanted to see a much heavier focus on the basic tools of reading—like phonics and spelling.

Grant says that PBS, CPB and the Department of Education put significant funding toward programming that would teach kids how to read—but that's not what *Reading Rainbow* was trying to do.

"*Reading Rainbow* taught kids why to read," Grant says. "You know, the love of reading—[the show] encouraged kids to pick up a book and to read."

—*NPR Morning Edition*, August 28, 2009

No one would argue that teaching children the mechanics of reading is a bad idea, but what will happen when we stop teaching kids *why* they should read? Motivationally speaking, it's the *why*—the Big Picture—that resonates with promotion-minded people, and young children are much more likely to be promotion-focused than the grown-ups at PBS and the Department of Education who are making well-intentioned but misguided decisions like these.

## How Shall I Compare Thee?

Imagine that someone has handed you one of those *Consumer Reports*–style charts, comparing the various attributes of five different automobiles (or mutual funds or vacation destinations). The different choices are listed at the top, forming the columns. The dimensions of comparison (e.g., fuel efficiency, legroom) are listed along the left, forming the rows. So the question is, how do *you* read charts like this?

If promotion-focused Ray were reading a chart like this that compared vacation destinations rather than automobiles, he would begin by looking at all the features of Paris—the rich cultural offerings, the gourmet dining, the hefty price tag—and then move on to take a closer look at Orlando—fun for the kids, cheap airfare, but not a particularly exotic locale—and so on. He would want to get a complete sense of what the experience in one destination would be like before doing the same thing for an alternative destination.

If prevention-focused Jon were doing the choosing, he would prefer to compare each destination on every dimension separately: How much will each one cost? What do they offer culturally? How is the food? Is it a good place for families?

If you look across each row one at a time, comparing every product along that single dimension before moving on to the next dimension like Jon would, that's called *attribute processing*. When comparing automobiles, first you look at each car's fuel efficiency, *then* each car's legroom, and so on, forming an impression as to which car is best as you go from attribute to attribute. If, on the other hand, you prefer to look at all the information about a single product, get an overall sense of it, and then move on to the next column like Ray does, that's called *holistic processing*. First you look at all the features of the Honda Civic, then the Hyundai Elantra, and so on, making a judgment of which car is best only once you've seen them all.

If you are prevention-focused, you generally prefer attribute processing, because it's careful and deliberate. It allows you to analyze your choices feature by feature and miss no small detail. Holistic processing, on the other hand, is usually preferred by the promotion-focused. This comparison method allows you, for each product, to take in the big picture and get an overall *feeling* about that product.

## Totally New or Tried-and-True?

Does the choice you are making involve trying something new? *Brand spanking* new? Because if it is, that's what promotion-focused people usually want. *Let's try that new restaurant across town. Let's redecorate the living room in the hot new colors. Hey, is that the new iPhone?* They are eager to choose something different from what they've chosen in the past, because new experiences mean new opportunities for advancements or gains. And as we've mentioned several times now, if there is anything a promotion-motivated person hates, it's a missed opportunity for gain. Promotion-minded people will, for instance, gladly trade in what they've already got for something new of equal value, or work to obtain a new prize rather than regain one that was lost. If you interrupt them in the middle of a task (say, a crossword puzzle), and then give them the option to finish the puzzle or switch to something else (say, Sudoku), most of the time they prefer to leave the puzzle in the past and see what Sudoku has to offer.[3] So you can expect them to make choices that bring about change.

The prevention-minded, on the other hand, don't care for change. They prefer stability, familiarity, and tradition. They thrive on knowing what to expect—that way, they can plan for every eventuality. New experiences are new opportunities, all right—they are opportunities *to make a mistake*. Prevention-minded people are reluctant to surrender the certainty of the known for the perils of the unknown. "You say this trade is for something of equal value," they think, "but is it *really*?" They will choose to keep what they already have, thank you very much. And they will finish that crossword puzzle, because things half done are half *un*done, and that's unacceptable.

## Walk on the Wild Side or on the Sidewalk

Everybody likes a big payoff, especially the promotion-minded. But not everyone is comfortable with the risks that big payoffs often entail—and when we say "not everyone," you know who we're talking about, don't you? So if you have to choose between a high-risk and a more conservative option, your dominant motivation is basically going to take charge. This is precisely why, for instance, prevention-focused investors choose annuities and CDs (certificates of deposit, not compact discs), rather than individual stocks or hedge funds. They are willing to accept the fact that their low-risk, low-reward annuity will probably never make them rich, in exchange for the peace of mind they get from knowing that their money is going to be there when they need it.

In the normal course of things, people with a promotion focus are more willing than those with a prevention focus to choose the risky option over a more conservative option. But there are, for the record, times when people with a strong prevention focus are more willing than anyone to choose the risky option. When prevention-focused people find themselves in trouble or in danger, they will do *anything necessary* to return to safety. They don't like the risky option, but they choose it nonetheless if it is the only way to return to a satisfactory safe state.[4] People are always surprised when they read a news story about a respected bank representative who risked and lost hundreds of millions of dollars of investment funds. Our guess is that this is a prevention-focused person desperately trying to restore an account that went sour. Unwilling to accept a small loss, the banker felt that taking a big risk was the only viable option . . . and when this failed it was necessary to take an even bigger risk . . . and so on and so on.

## Listening to Your Head or Your Heart

There is a show on HGTV called *House Hunters*. Each episode follows an individual or couple looking to buy a new home as they tour three different options and ultimately choose their favorite. (There is also a version called *House Hunters International*, where you can watch Americans buying homes overseas become visibly shaken by the small size of European kitchens and bathrooms.)

At the end of the show, after revealing the chosen home, the buyers talk about how they ultimately made their decision. Some focus on the specific features that sealed the deal:

*It had the square footage we were looking for.*
*We really wanted an en suite bathroom and a big backyard.*
*With this home, we were able to stay within our budget.*

Others emphasize their personal, emotional reaction to the house:

*I walked in and knew immediately I was home.*
*It has a warm, happy feeling to it.*
*This house is just so "us."*

When forming an opinion, promotion-minded people tend to rely more on their subjective experience—*their feelings*—as a guide. They are the ones picking the house because of its "good vibes." If promotion-focused people feel good (e.g., happier, excited, cheerful) when looking at an advertisement or listening to their boss's motivational pep talk, then they are more likely to be persuaded by it. To use a *Star Trek* analogy, they think like Captain Kirk and go with their "gut."

Prevention-minded people are more like Spock. They prefer logic and reason and rely more on the *substance* of a message or argument to form opinions.[5] These are the people who buy a house because it meets a particular set of objective criteria—the right size, location, number of bathrooms, and amount of strain on their wallets. If the reasons for doing something are solid, they are willing to do it. (It's not that they don't *have* feelings—they just think feelings are not a sound basis for a good decision.)

## How Long Will This Take?

Figuring out how much time a project or task is going to take to complete is a big factor when you're deciding whether or not to do it.

> Wife: *How do you feel about repainting the kitchen this weekend?*
> Husband: *Ugh. How long is that going to take? The playoffs are on!*

> Prospective student: *Wait, it takes how many years to get a PhD? Seriously?*

> Traveler: *Taking the subway to the airport is cheaper, but the ride is so long. When will I need to leave to get there on time?*

The problem is, people aren't very good at estimating how long things will take. Psychologists refer to this as the *planning fallacy*, and it has the very real potential to mess up our decisions and keep us from reaching our goals.

Studies show that the planning fallacy can be attributed to several different biases we have when estimating how long it will take to do just about anything. First, we routinely fail to consider our own past experiences while planning. When your husband tells you it will take him fifteen minutes to vacuum the carpets, he is probably ignoring the fact that it took him an hour to do it last time. And as any professor can tell you, most college seniors, after four straight years of paper writing, still can't seem to figure out how long it will take them to write a ten-page paper. We just don't take our past into account the way we should when thinking about our future.

Second, we ignore the very real possibility that things won't go as planned—our future plans tend to be "best-case scenarios." (Naturally, the optimistic/promotion-focused have particular trouble with this one.) So running to the store for a new vacuum cleaner might take fifteen minutes—if there is no traffic, if they carry the model you're looking for, if you find it right away, and if there aren't long lines at the register. But we usually just assume that everything will go according to plan and will take fifteen minutes, even though it usually won't.

Last, we don't think about all the steps or subcomponents that make up the task, and consider how long *each part* of the task will take. When you think about painting a room, you may picture yourself using a roller to quickly slap the paint on the walls, and think that it won't take much time at all—neglecting to consider how you'll first have to move or cover the furniture, tape all the fixtures and window frames, do all the edging by hand, and so on.

Promotion-focused people are more likely to ignore potential snags and less likely to break things down into the nitty-gritty steps of reaching the goal, so they routinely underestimate how long things will take. The prevention-minded do this to some extent as well, but less so—since they have a natural inclination to consider what might go wrong each step of the way.

## What We Buy

When you see the world in terms of accomplishment versus safety, you shop differently. Your dominant motivational focus determines not only the kinds of products you find appealing, but the particular attributes of a product that grab your attention. For instance, MSC Fellow Jens Förster has found that promotion-focused people tend to want products that are advertised as luxurious or comfortable, because they provide *positives*. When choosing among sunglasses and wristwatches, promotion-minded participants in one of his studies were most influenced by features like "fashionable earpieces" and "time zone settings"—attributes that are hardly necessary but convey a sense of coolness or sophistication. The red sports car, the hot tub, the Chanel bag, the three-hundred-dollar bottle of wine—no matter what you may tell yourself if you buy one, no one has ever truly *needed* any of these items. But if you are promotion-focused, odds are good that you *want* at least one of them.

Prevention-focused people, on other hand, want to avoid *negatives*—so they seek products advertised as safe and secure. In Förster's study they preferred sunglasses with a "long guarantee period" and wristwatches with "secure buckles." (Not exactly exciting stuff, but then excitement isn't really the point.) In another study, prevention-minded participants preferred washing machines advertised with the slogans "established for many years" and "consumer tests prove: safe and reliable" over promotion-focused models that had "the newest technology available" and "lots of new functions."[6]

An early MSC study conducted by Diane Safer provides another illustration of how focus influences our purchasing decisions. Undergraduates were told to imagine that they wanted to buy a computer (with cost not an issue). They were provided a list of twenty-four questions about a computer and were asked to read all of them and then select those ten questions that they believed would be most helpful in making their purchase decision. Of the twenty-four questions, eight were computer attributes having to do with innovation (e.g., how creative or advanced it was) and eight were computer attributes having to do with reliability (e.g., its ability to stop system crashes or other problems), with the remaining eight attributes having to do with other concerns (e.g., total weight of the unit). Those individuals who had a stronger promotion focus were more likely to seek information concerning innovation than reliability, whereas those with a stronger prevention focus were more likely to seek information concerning reliability than innovation.[7]

Incidentally, promotion-focused people don't just like *new* products, like the latest version of the iPhone or Prius—they are also big fans of what marketers call *really new* products—those that represent a whole new category of thing that's never been available before, like the Segway (and, once upon a time, the DustBuster, Sony Walkman, and Apple personal computer). It might be more accurate to say they are the *only* fans of such products, since your average prevention-minded person isn't going to shell out her hard-earned money for something that has no track record. Prevention-focused people prefer established products—the ones we consider "essential." (Note that, thanks to the Internet, a personal computer is now considered essential in many households—which is why prevention-minded people have gotten on board and bought them. After they've read all the negative reviews to check on their reliability, that is.)

In case you are worried that promotion-motivated people are naïve suckers who will buy anything so long as it's shiny, don't be—just like their more cautious counterparts, they can be sensitive to the potential problems associated with really new products. But only if you point them out, or if the context makes the potential problems obvious—promotion-minded people are less likely to consider them spontaneously.[8] Which is why every promotion-focused person would be wise to take a more prevention-minded friend with him to the mall—like a buddy system that keeps your money from getting lost.

It's also important to always keep in mind that, even though you have a dominant focus, it can change from moment to moment depending on the situation you're in—and consequently your purchase preferences and comfort with risk can change, too. For example, *what* you are buying can trigger a particular motivation—if you want a product that will keep your children from getting to poisonous cleaning products, you will be prevention-focused while making your choice, because it's a decision that is inherently about safety and danger. You will want the established and reliable cabinet lock, and you won't care much about how fashionable or innovative it may be. Similarly, a promotion-focused person may buy herself a flashy red sports car with lots of bells and whistles, but when it comes to buying her teenager *her* first car, chances are this parent will be thinking about antilock brakes and airbags.

We should also note that it's perfectly possible that promotion- and prevention-minded shoppers will make the *same* choice in a given situation. For instance, why did you buy this book? Did you feel it would offer you something new, something that you hoped would help you to make progress personally or professionally? Or were you thinking that you really ought to read it, particularly since it is filled with the kind of data-driven, science-based arguments you generally find convincing? Different motivations can lead us to make the same choice, albeit for different reasons, based on different features. (By the way—whatever your reasons . . . *good choice.*)

## That Might Work on Them, but You Can't Fool Me

No one knows better than a social psychologist (which, if we didn't make it clear already, happens to be what we are) that you can't manipulate people into doing something if they *know* that you are manipulating them. If we brought undergraduate participants into the lab and said, "We are going to say and do a few things that are going to put you into a promotion focus, and then show that you are more likely to buy this *luxurious* foot cream over this *reliable* pumice stone since promotion-focused people like luxury," here's roughly what would happen:

- 40 percent would buy the foot cream, because they either (1) want to give the "right" answer or (2) are trying to be helpful
- 40 percent would buy the pumice stone, because they either (1) don't like being told what to do or (2) are trying to be deliberately unhelpful
- 20 percent would fall asleep or start texting friends . . . because that always happens anyhow

This is why research psychologists provide introductions to our studies that do not tell participants everything about what we're manipulating and what effect we expect. The same thing can be said of people in the persuasion business, like advertisers and political operatives. Sometimes you know what they are doing, but they would really prefer that you didn't—because the manipulation works more effectively when you don't.

Given their focus on what might go wrong, it won't surprise you to learn that the prevention-focused are more sensitive to, and more actively on guard against, being manipulated or persuaded. Studies show them to be more skeptical from the outset and more likely to pick up on subtle signs of manipulation. Their suspicion is quickly aroused when advertisers claim that consumers preferred their product to "the leading brand" without naming *which* brand it was, or when the company that manufactures the product conducted the test (rather than an objective evaluator, like *Consumer Reports*). So as a group, the prevention-minded are a bit more difficult to manipulate.[9] And if you are a car salesman, these are the people who will walk into your showroom and absolutely ruin your day by telling you what they expect to pay and what they expect to get for it.

## Let It Go, Man

Sometimes you really should throw in the towel. As time passes, it becomes clear that you've made a bad choice and things aren't working out as you planned. You realize that pursuing whatever it is that you're pursuing, whether it's being successful in your current career, mending a troubled dating relationship, or renovating your house from top to bottom, will cost you too much financially or emotionally, or take too long. Do you move on to new opportunities, or simply stay the course and sacrifice your own well-being in the process?

For many of us, the answer is "stay the course." And everyone, at one time or another, has known what it's like to stay in a job or a relationship long after it has ceased being satisfying, or to take on a project that's just too big for us and be reluctant to admit it. CEOs have been known to allocate manpower and money to projects long after it's become clear that they are obviously failing, digging a deeper hole rather than trying to climb their way out of it. (Remember how long it took to get rid of New Coke?)

The costs to people who can't bring themselves to move on, in terms of time, effort, and lost opportunities for a better life, can be enormous. We recognize this kind of foolishness immediately in others, but that doesn't stop us from making the same mistake ourselves. *Why?*

There are several powerful and largely unconscious psychological forces at work here. We may throw good money after bad, or waste time in a dead-end relationship, because we haven't come up with an alternative, or because we don't want to admit to our friends or family . . . or ourselves, that we were wrong. But the most likely culprit is our overwhelming aversion to *sunk costs*.

Sunk costs, as we discussed in the last chapter, are the resources that you've put into an endeavor that you can't get back. They are the years you spent training for a profession you hate or waiting for your commitment-phobic boyfriend to propose. They are the money you spent on redecorating your living room in the hot new style, only to find that you hate living in it.

Once you've realized that you probably won't succeed or that you are unhappy with the results, it shouldn't matter how much time and effort you've already put into something. If your job or your boyfriend have taken up some of the best years of your life, it doesn't make sense to let them use up the years you've got left. And an ugly living room is an ugly room to live in, no matter how much money you spent making it so.

The problem is that it doesn't *feel* that way. Putting in a lot only to end up with nothing to show for it is just too awful for most of us to consider seriously. We worry far too much about what we'll lose if we just move on, and not nearly enough about the costs of *not* moving on—more wasted time and effort, more distress, and more missed opportunities. So how can we make it easier to know when to cut our losses?

Thanks to recent research by Northwestern University psychologist and MSC Fellow Daniel Molden, there is a simple and effective way to be sure you are making the best decisions when things go awry: be promotion-focused about it. People who have a dominant promotion motivation, or who adopt a promotion focus with respect to the problem (something we'll show you how to do in chapter 8), are more comfortable with making mistakes and accepting the losses they may have to incur along the way. They are more willing to give up on the status quo and move on.

For example, in one study, Molden asked each participant to imagine that he or she was president of an aviation company that had committed $10 million to developing a plane that can't be detected by radar. With the project near completion and $9 million already spent, a rival company announces the availability of their own radar-blank plane, which is both superior in performance *and* lower in cost. The question put to participants was simple—do you invest the remaining $1 million and finish your company's (inferior and more expensive) plane, or cut your losses and move on?

He found that prevention-focused participants stayed the course and invested the remaining $1 million *roughly 80 percent of the time*. They wanted to try to keep waging a losing battle. The odds of making that mistake were significantly reduced by having a promotion focus—those participants invested the remaining $1 million less than 60 percent of the time. So when we see our goals in terms of what we can gain, rather than of what we might lose, we are more likely to see a doomed endeavor for what it is, and move on and move forward to alternative possibilities for gain.

People don't really make strictly rational decisions—this much we know for certain. But our preferences and choices aren't random, either—they are based on biases that are systematic and predictable. Making *good* choices often involves being able to recognize your own biases and, when necessary, compensate for them. When you are promotion-focused, you need to remember that you tend to weigh the pros more than the cons, that you probably underestimate the time it takes to do things, and that you are less likely to realize you're being manipulated by an advertisement or a salesperson. When you are prevention-focused, you may limit your options unnecessarily, overweigh the cons, and have a hard time knowing when to throw in the towel when something isn't working. Recognizing your biases is the first, essential step in overcoming them—now you know what to be on the lookout for.

# CHAPTER 7

# Focus on Our World

WHAT KIND OF SOCIETY SHOULD WE LIVE IN, AND WHAT SHOULD our priorities be? Who should be in charge, and whom should we vote for (or against)? What should be changed, if anything? Our answers to these questions are shaped by many influences. They will depend on the culture in which we are raised, our early upbringing, the kind of education we receive, our religious beliefs, and of course, our personal experiences. They will also depend, in part, on whether we see the world as a place filled with opportunities for gain or as a place filled with the potential for loss. No understanding of how human beings relate to one another—person to person, ethnic group to ethnic group, or nation to nation—could be complete without considering the motivational focus lenses that different people look through.

## The Right Way to Run Things

Why do you vote the way you do, or give donations to some candidates and not others? Particularly in the United States, we tend to see our political views as essentially products of *ideology*—as a reflection of our sense of not only how the world actually works, but how it would work best. For instance, if you are someone who believes that in a well-run society, people need to pay higher taxes to support social programs, or efforts like affirmative action are needed to ensure equal access to opportunity, you probably think of yourself as a Democrat or a Liberal. If you are someone who believes that in a well-run society, people should pay lower taxes, be subject to less government regulation, and embrace more personal responsibility, you probably think of yourself as a Republican or a Conservative. You may be surprised to learn that your political views are also shaped, at least in part, by your dominant motivational focus.

When people are promotion-focused, as we learned in the previous chapter, they are more likely to support change they see as an advancement—to long for such change, in fact. It's natural for the promotion-minded, then, to favor reform or progressivism over appeals to the status quo or conservativism. (Note the small *p* and *c* in *progressivism* and *conservativism*. We're not talking about allegiance with particular political parties. Remember that historically, there have been reforms proposed by both Republicans, e.g., social security reform, *and* Democrats, e.g., health care reform, and both parties have been known to issue vigorous defenses of the status quo. In point of fact, being promotion-focused makes you only slightly more likely to be a Democrat politically, and prevention-focused people can be found in roughly equal numbers in both parties.)[1] Of course, just like an effective workplace or marriage, a wise government will contain a balance of perspectives, as famously illustrated by Abraham Lincoln's "Team of Rivals."

One particularly interesting study that nicely illustrates how promotion and prevention shape our political views presented Australian voters with a (hypothetical) referendum on risky sweeping economic reforms—ones that had never before been tried, but had big potential benefits. Promotion-focused voters consistently chose to go with reform, and they did so even when the current economic situation wasn't particularly dire—in other words, when reforms weren't in any sense necessary. Prevention-focused voters, on the other hand, preferred keeping the current system—even when a new approach was truly called for.[2]

Even though dominant motivations are relatively stable for any given individual, significant changes in a country's political or economic circumstances are capable of bringing about large shifts in the motivational focus of its citizens as a whole. In times of prosperity, growth, and peace, people are likely to be more promotion-focused. When jobs are plentiful and market indices keep rising, people are open to change, more comfortable with risk, and optimistic about the future. Since the United States, in its short history as a nation, has known relatively more prosperity, growth, and peace than many other countries, it makes sense that the American culture is so particularly promotion-focused. It is known, after all, as the "Land of Opportunity." It really doesn't get more promotion-focused than that.

But of course things haven't always been rosy in the United States—there have been economic recessions and depressions, times when jobs were scarce, and years when the country has been at war. At the time we are writing this, there have been six U.S. presidents who ran for reelection during wartime (the last was George W. Bush). *Every single one* was reelected—even when the wars were unpopular ones. Now that you know so much about prevention motivation, you can see why that would be true. When our national sense of security is threatened and people are struggling to get by, we are a lot less willing to take a gamble on a new and untested candidate. We don't want any more ugly surprises. We stick with the leader we have, even if we aren't all that crazy about him. Stability is a source of comfort. Plus, it's one less thing to worry about.

There are times, of course, when promotion- and prevention-focused people will get behind different political candidates or come down on opposite sides of an issue. But many political issues can be "spun" in different ways, so the same vote or course of action can appear to serve either motivation. Take the issue of "Big Government"—or how much government officials should meddle in the lives of the citizenry. Promotion motivation leads to support for government interventions when they are described as ensuring opportunities for *growth* and *enrichment*, but for the prevention-focused, such an appeal falls on deaf ears. On the other hand, prevention motivation leads to strong support for the very same programs when they are instead described as maintaining *public and personal safety* (or *defense capabilities*).[3]

So when people are focused on what they have to gain, they are most persuaded by political messages that offer change, improvement, and a better life. But when they are focused on maintaining nonloss, they may fear change (even when change could be helpful) and will be most interested in political messages that appeal to their need for greater security and maintaining the status quo. If you are a politician trying to drum up support for your legislation among voters, it's important to always remember that you have *two* constituencies, and they will need to be convinced in very different ways.

## Who Votes?

In the United States, roughly 60 percent of eligible voters turn up to vote in presidential election years. That number drops to about 40 percent for midterm elections. In terms of demographics, we know that younger people are, on average, less likely to vote, and that seniors are more likely to do so. Women are also a bit more likely to vote than men. But what role, if any, does our dominant motivation play?

There is no reason to believe that either promotion- or prevention-focused people care more about the political, economic, and social issues that affect our lives. You might expect one group or the other to care more about *specific* issues, like national security (prevention) or equal access to opportunity (promotion), but not to care more across the board. So you would think that the voter turnout in each group would be about the same. Surprisingly, the promotion-minded among us are actually more likely to get themselves to the polls and vote. Why might that be?

On the surface, it doesn't seem to make sense—after all, shouldn't the people who see everything as a potential threat, and rely on government to help keep them out of danger, care *a lot* about who governs them? They do, but they stay home anyway. The problem is that voting is—strategically speaking—an *eager* behavior. You are going out of your way to vote *for* someone, to help him or her *win*. Promotion-minded people love winning, and love to do things that make winning happen—so voting feels right to them, and worth the effort of standing in a long line during their lunch break.

If, however, you make it possible for people to vote *against* someone or something, then the prevention-minded start showing up in droves. They are more than willing, for instance, to show up for referendums. Most referendums make a "no" vote possible, by asking citizens to either support or reject a change to current law. Voting against something is a vigilant behavior—it keeps something bad from happening, and that's what prevention is all about. This is perhaps why so many conservative politicians in the 2012 national election campaign emphasized the importance of voting against President Obama, rather than voting for the Republican presidential candidate. So, understanding a little bit about how promotion and prevention work, a clever candidate will campaign not only on all the compelling reasons why you should vote *for* her, but also on the reasons why you must vote *against* her opponent (by voting for her, of course).[4] For example, if you can convince prevention-focused voters that the current state of the nation is terrible, or even that the nation is in present danger, then they will treat voting against the responsible incumbent as a necessity to save the country and restore it to safety. Rather than protecting the status quo as they usually do, they will take a chance and vote to change who is in power.

## The Perils of Power

History shows us that being in the majority tends to have a lot of good things going for it. The majority (usually, though not always) holds the most power, hogs the most resources, and gets to dictate the rules by which everyone else has to live. If you are a member of the majority, these sound like the sort of circumstances that might make you focused on gain, since you have so many more opportunities at your fingertips than those in the minority do.

But did you ever notice how *nervous* people in the majority seem to be about the minority? For example—take the current controversy over U.S. immigration. According to data collected by the Pew Research Center, more than half of non-Hispanic white Americans believe that "growing immigration threatens traditional American culture and values" and that "immigrants today are a burden because they take jobs, housing, etc."—this despite the fact that only 14 percent say they have actually lost a job to an immigrant.[5]

"There's a real perception among some Americans right now that immigration is suddenly at their front door," said David A. Shirk, director of the Trans-Border Institute at the University of San Diego. "They are not used to it. They are not convinced that those groups are going to effectively assimilate. And they are very concerned that our way of life in the United States is going to have to change as a result of that."[6]

*Los Angeles Times*, May 1, 2008

Throughout human history, minority groups have been viewed as threats to the majority. From the Jews in Europe to the Christians in the Middle East to gay men and women just about everywhere, minorities have been labeled as dangerous and destructive and thought to be actively plotting the majority's ultimate demise. We can see evidence of this kind of thinking in some Americans' attitudes toward our own growing Muslim minority:

More than a dozen American states are considering outlawing aspects of Shariah law. Some of these efforts would curtail Muslims from settling disputes over dietary laws and marriage through religious arbitration, while others would go even further in stigmatizing Islamic life: a bill recently passed by the Tennessee General Assembly equates Shariah with a set of rules that promote "the destruction of the national existence of the United States."

Supporters of these bills contend that such measures are needed to protect the country against homegrown terrorism and safeguard its Judeo-Christian values. The Republican presidential candidate Newt Gingrich has said that "Shariah is a mortal threat to the survival of freedom in the United States and in the world as we know it."

—Eliyahu Stern, Yale professor of religious studies and history[7]

It turns out that majority thinking tends to be a lot more prevention-focused than you might expect it to be. The majority is worried, because it basically has nowhere to go but down. And the status quo is working well for them . . . so well that they want to maintain it. So members of the majority often become highly motivated to hold on to what they've got. It's actually *minority* group thinking that is promotion-focused. Because they lack power (relatively speaking), they have nowhere to go but *up*. The status quo is not working well for them, so they want change that will advance their position in society. The journey to getting power, to making progress, is a promotion journey, but once you've arrived, staying in power is all about preventing other people from taking your power away.

There are times, however, when members of the minority group shift and aren't so promotion-minded. Being treated unfairly because you belong to a minority, or even being reminded of your stigmatized social status (i.e., that your group is thought of as somehow inferior), can create a state of threat, which increases your prevention focus. This happens not only to members of minority racial and ethnic groups when dealing with majority whites, but to women working in majority-male environments (or really anyone working in any context in which they feel their group is outnumbered and undervalued). Under these kinds of circumstances, the minority member is likely to be more pessimistic, cautious, and risk averse—and a bit more likely to interpret something ambiguous, like being ignored by a preoccupied coworker or classmate, as negative.[8]

## Us versus Them, or Me versus You?

One of the most interesting, and psychologically important, ways in which cultures differ from one another has to do with how they view the "self." In other words, how do you define "you"? (This can be a little hard to wrap your head around—we are each so used to thinking *one* way about what a "self" is that it never really occurs to us that there might be *another* way to think about it.)

In Western countries (and nowhere more so than in the United States), we have what psychologists call an *independent* view of the self. In other words, only you are "you." You might have intimate relationships with other people, belong to groups that are important to you, but none of that fits into the definition of what "you" are. The independent view of the self has very distinct boundaries—you are you, and everyone else is *not* you. This view leads naturally to an emphasis on *personal* goals, wishes, and desires. The *independent* culture supports valuing autonomy and individual achievement first and foremost, fostering (on average) more promotion motivation.

## Independent View of the Self

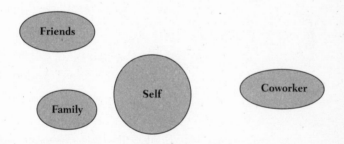

Others vary in closeness with the self, but never are included within the self-concept.

In Asian or Eastern cultures (and also in much of South American culture), the view of the self is more *interdependent*. Our most important relationships constitute a part of who we are—so much so that our successes and failures don't simply reflect on our family or group, but they *belong* to these people as well. For example, psychologists studying Chinese culture have found that the Chinese, compared to Westerners, place a far greater emphasis on sharing the rewards of individual success with the group. Not surprisingly, Chinese students often emphasize the driving force of their family and community when explaining their motivation to achieve.[9] The academic success of the child is an important source of pride for his or her entire family, and academic failure is a source of family shame.

Cultures that foster an interdependent self-concept tend to place a lot of emphasis on responsibility, duty, and obligation to the group. They value fitting in harmoniously and being someone everyone else can count on, rather than standing out and doing things "your way." Not surprisingly, people raised in these cultures tend to be more prevention motivated than their Western peers.[10]

### Interdependent View of the Self

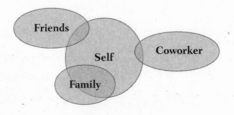

Others vary in closeness with the self, and are included within the self-concept.

Of course, there are many individuals in any culture who don't hold the prevailing view—Americans who are more *inter*dependent by nature, and Chinese who are more *in*dependent. Also, gender plays a role—women in every culture have, on average, a more interdependent view of themselves than men. And there are times when even a person who has a strong independent self may become more interdependent—for instance, when participating on a sports team or a work team that has shared outcomes.

Because prevention-focused people are a bit more interdependent, and include important others within their self-boundary, they tend to think in more "us versus them" terms. If you threaten to harm a prevention-focused person, he will probably (and understandably) feel a mixture of anxiety and dread, triggering some kind of flight response. In other words, he is going to want to get away from the harm. But threaten to harm his group or another group member, and you'll have some serious trouble on your hands. His response shifts from flight to *fight*. When the prevention-minded take action to protect their group (or the cultural practices and values of the group), they do so not only from a desire to protect, but also from a sense of moral conviction—from the belief that fighting is the *right* thing to do. They are also more willing than their promotion-focused peers to endorse doing harm to "them" for injuries done to "us."[11] To illustrate what we're talking about, one need look no further than the example of the otherwise gentle and unintimidating mother who is prepared to attack to protect her young child.

Promotion-focused people are more individualistic and tend to think in more "me versus you" terms. They are more interested in retaliating for injuries inflicted upon them personally than the prevention-minded are, and less likely to want to seek vengeance for an injury perpetrated on the group.[12]

## Why Birds of a Feather Flock Together

Most people don't realize it, but one of the strongest predictors of how much you like something—or someone—is simple familiarity. People just naturally like things that they have seen before (something psychologists call the *mere exposure effect*). This kind of process is largely unconscious, so you don't have to be aware of the fact that you've seen something before in order to like it more. For instance, in one study researchers varied the number of times a particular student attended different lecture courses as a visitor. At the end of the semester, the students in the different classes were shown a picture of the visitor and were asked to rate how likable the person seemed. The students rated her as significantly more likable when she had attended their class ten to fifteen times than when she had attended their class only five or fewer times—even though *none* of the students consciously recalled ever having seen her in class.[13]

A sense of familiarity doesn't just come from having seen someone before. Even a stranger can seem familiar to us if they share our appearance, background, attitudes, or political views. This is part of the reason why we tend to like people who belong to our in-group more than people from the out-group—they are usually more similar to us, and therefore more familiar.

Of course, familiarity is but one of the reasons why we like people who think, look, and act the way we do. Another is *social validation*—a kind of confirmation that our characteristics or beliefs are the right ones or the best ones. Human beings naturally turn to one another for this kind of information, since there often is no objective criterion we might use to judge ourselves or our actions. So we look around, see what other people are doing, and use that as a guide. Similar others do the same things we do, so they make us feel good about ourselves.

Dissimilarity, on the other hand, is disturbing. Why does the other group think that X is the right thing to do, when my group thinks Y is? Assuming that you believe X and Y can't both be right or best, these kinds of thoughts create an unpleasant mental state of tension that psychologists call *cognitive dissonance*, because they seem to directly conflict with one another. The easiest way to resolve the problem and rid yourself of the dissonance is to conclude that the other group is wrong. And if people are running around doing wrongheaded things, then it's easy to start drawing negative inferences about them (e.g., "they're crazy," "they're stupid").

Our dominant motivational focus affects these interpersonal processes in a couple of ways. First, and perhaps most obviously, it forms a *basis* of similarity. If you are promotion-focused, you are more likely to see yourself and your own perspective in the attitude and behavior of other promotion-focused people—your fellow risk takers, idealists, and optimists. The prevention-minded, on the other hand, will see a kindred spirit in the cautious, responsible, and principled realists. Now, these are people I can understand!

Second, our dominant focus affects how we interact with similar others (in-group members) and dissimilar ones (out-group members). The more promotion-focused you are, the more you want to approach other in-group members and form close bonds, because these are the people who will most likely provide you with opportunities to gain something: friendship, social support, connections, and so on. The motto is "Promote Us." The more prevention-focused you are, the more you want to avoid out-group members as much as possible, because these are the people that you can least trust—the people who are most likely to disagree with you or possibly do you harm. The motto is "Prevent Them."

Interestingly, you can even see these tendencies reflected in things like where we choose to sit. When undergraduates were told that a seat with a backpack on it in the psychology lab belonged to their in-group member (i.e., a teammate), those with a strong promotion focus chose a seat closer to the backpack than those with a weak promotion focus. (Prevention focus had nothing to do with how close they sat to the in-group member.) But when the backpack belonged to an out-group member (i.e., a competitor), it was having a strong prevention focus that led students to choose a seat farther away from it. (Promotion focus had nothing to do with how far away they sat from the out-group member.) So when it comes to favoring your group over others, the promotion- and prevention-minded show their biases in very different ways—promoting *us* versus preventing *them*.[14]

## The Challenge to All Get Along

Most of us agree (at least when we're asked publicly) that the world would be a better place without prejudice and discrimination. People have the right to be judged for who they are based on their own actions, not by the actions of the group to which they belong or the reputation of their group (often misleading or out-and-out false). But thanks to the human brain's tendency to automatically categorize everything it sees, judging others fairly and without preconceived notions turns out to be a bigger challenge than many people acknowledge.

There is a fundamental reason for this: categorization is an incredibly useful thing. By grouping similar things, we are able to know immediately how to interact with something we've never actually seen before. When you see a chair, you know you are supposed to sit on it, without consulting a manual, even though you've never sat on that particular chair. When you bite into an apple, you know you are going to get an experience that tastes like an apple rather than a cabbage or an onion, without having to "test" the apple first in any way. You only need to taste *one* apple, in fact, to know what all the rest of them will basically taste like, because your brain creates a category "apple" that you can use to guide your fruit purchases from now on. That's the essential benefit of learning from past experience.

Because categorization is so time-saving (and sometimes, lifesaving—as in, don't eat *that kind* of mushroom because last time it made you sick), our brains evolved to categorize rapidly and efficiently, without any conscious intent on our part. This is mostly a good thing—except when it comes to categorizing people, rather than apples. This is where we can get into trouble, and why stereotypes get activated in our minds even when we are trying to avoid using them to judge someone we've just met. Psychologists call this *implicit bias*, and they have struggled for years to come up with ways to successfully combat its influence on our thoughts and behavior.

They wondered, for instance, if the best way to cope with implicit bias was to tell people to try to be *egalitarian* (i.e., treat all people equally) and help bring about racial *harmony*, or, alternatively, to try to *avoid bias* and prevent racial *discord*. Which is more effective? (You see this one coming a mile away, don't you?) As it happens, the effectiveness of the strategy depends a lot on your dominant motivation. Promotion-focused people show less prejudice on implicit measures of racial bias—ones they can't consciously control—when they are told to strive to be egalitarian and contribute to harmony. Prevention-focused people, on the other hand, are less biased when instructed to avoid bias and prevent discord.

Appeals to egalitarianism or to avoiding bias can also be made more or less effective depending on the context in which you present them. In one study, researchers varied whether the slogan "Say Yes to Equality" or "Say No to Prejudice" appeared over a set of positive images (e.g., black and white children playing together; a smiling mixed-race family; black and white hands clasped together; a photo of Dr. Martin Luther King) or negative images (e.g., white-robed KKK members; a burning cross; police striking civil rights demonstrators). They found that for the promotion focused, saying yes to equality was much more persuasive in the more positive context, while for prevention-focused people, saying no to prejudice was more compelling in the negative context.[15]

## What Happens When Your Beliefs About a Group Are Disconfirmed?

What happens when someone surprises you by acting in a way that's completely inconsistent with the stereotype of his or her group? When you meet a female math genius, a male nurse, an African American CEO, or an Asian American basketball sensation? Generally speaking, when the world doesn't quite work the way we expect it to work, it's a little disconcerting. We count on our environment—which includes the people in it—to be a largely predictable place, so we can make plans and feel confident that we can handle whatever comes our way. How would you react to an apple-looking fruit that tasted like a shrimp?

Disconfirmation of a belief—even a stereotypic belief—is threatening. You may not be able to consciously detect it, but psychologists can with the use of sophisticated tools that measure heart rate, skin conductance, and stress hormones like cortisol. On a deeper level than you may realize, it feels very unsettling to have your expectations disconfirmed. In order to get rid of this feeling of threat, the most common response is to try to ignore the information that caused it—which is part of why stereotypes can persist in the face of so much evidence that they are substantially wrong.

Prevention-minded people, not surprisingly, experience more anxiety when someone violates their expectations. But far from ignoring it, studies have found that they actually have *better* memory for the inconsistent behavior. In fact, studies show that prevention-focused people are more likely to want to spend time with and really get to know the person whose attributes or behavior called their beliefs into question because they want to try to understand where they went wrong and what their correct belief should be.[16] They want to meet the female math genius or black CEO and walk away secure in the knowledge that they've gotten a better handle on things. So even though prevention-focused people are a bit more likely to avoid members of the out-group, they are the ones most likely to pay attention when they are wrong about an out-group member and will try to get it right.

Promotion and prevention focus give us powerful insights into some of the most important social questions of our age. What social policies should be changed, if any? How do the people with power feel about the people who lack it but want more of it? How can citizens be persuaded to vote more, and for whom (or against whom)? How do we see our "self," and to what extent are the groups to which we belong part of our "self"? How do we treat people who belong to groups other than our own, and how can we most effectively overcome obstacles to social harmony like stereotyping and prejudice? To find the answers, our politicians, activists, and educators would be wise to keep motivational focus in mind.

# CHAPTER 8

## Identifying and Changing Focus

BY NOW YOU HAVE NO DOUBT GOTTEN A PRETTY FIRM HANDLE ON whether you are more promotion- or prevention-focused. But how can you identify someone *else's* motivation, so you can assign them to the right kinds of work, or so you can tailor your message content and delivery for maximum effectiveness? The "someone else" in question could be your spouse, your employee, your child, your student, your constituents, or the potential consumers you hope will buy your product. In most cases, it probably won't be practical for you to hand out the questionnaires we use at the MSC to determine motivational focus. Instead, we'll show you how you can use information like age, culture, personal values, and occupation to make highly educated and accurate guesses.

We'll also teach you how to look for the telltale clues: Does your employee care more about climbing the corporate ladder or hanging on to his job? Does your target consumer care more about bells and whistles or reliability and low cost? Does your teenager seem to be listening when you tell him smoking is dangerous? Does your risk-averse boss embrace your ideas for innovation? Even the sports we play and the expressions we use in everyday conversation reveal something about how we are motivated.

Getting at your audience's dominant focus is important, because people are more motivated by promises that *feel right* to them. They are more persuaded by arguments and ideas that are expressed in *their* motivational language. But before you can do that, you need to know which language to use for each particular person or audience.

## Clues from Age

It won't surprise you to learn that promotion-mindedness is most prevalent among the young.[1] Youth is a time for focusing on your hopes for the future, what you *ideally* want to do—you don't have much in the way of responsibilities, and you still believe you can do anything you set your mind to. Oh, and you think you are immortal. This is more or less a recipe for strong promotion motivation.

As we get older, our motivation starts to shift. Suddenly there is a mortgage that needs to be paid, a home that must be maintained, and children to care for. (Speaking of children, new mothers are an especially prevention-minded group. They have the daunting task of somehow protecting a completely vulnerable, clueless, yet hell-bent-on-exploration infant from a world filled with germs, stairs, pointy objects, and electrical outlets. New motherhood is mostly about ceaseless vigilance.)

The older we get, the more we want to hang on to what we've already got—the things we've worked so hard to achieve. We also have more experience with pain and loss, having been knocked around a bit by life and having learned a few lessons the hard way. Consequently, we are more likely as we age to approach our goals with a prevention mindset.

You can see these age-related differences in motivation very much reflected in the workplace, where satisfaction with job security and flexible work schedules predict commitment for older workers, while opportunities to develop skills and linking salary increases to performance enhances commitment for people under thirty.[2]

## Clues from Culture

As we mentioned in the previous chapter, Americans (and Westerners more generally) tend to have a more independent view of the self and consequently are more promotion focused when it comes to their goals. East Asian and South American cultures foster a greater sense of interdependence and responsibility to the group, and therefore greater prevention focus.

Even within a single country there can be regions with different cultural norms—different ways of seeing and doing things. For instance, people living in the Pacific Northwest of the United States (i.e., Northern California, Washington, and Oregon) are relatively more promotion-focused, whereas those living in the Midwest are relatively more prevention-focused. And Hispanics are relatively more prevention motivated than other ethnicities in America.[3]

Wherever you see people living in close-knit communities, living according to fairly prescribed (and largely agreed-upon) ways of doing things, expect there to be a stronger prevention focus. Where people are less connected to one another, and where basically "anything goes," expect to find more promotion focus.

## Clues from Careers and Sports

The promotion-minded and prevention-minded seem naturally drawn to different kinds of careers. Those with more prevention motivation are more likely to take up what organizational psychologists call "conventional and realistic" pursuits, fulfilling roles as administrators, bookkeepers, accountants, technicians, and manufacturing workers. These are occupations that require knowledge of rules and regulations, careful execution, and a propensity for thoroughness—the kinds of jobs where attention to detail is what really pays off.

The promotion-focused, on the other hand, are more likely to pursue "artistic and investigative" careers, as music teachers, copywriters, inventors, and consultants. These are more "think-outside-the-box" jobs, where people are rewarded for creative and innovative thinking, and there is less emphasis on being practical.

The promotion- and prevention-focused choose these different professions in part because they are driven by different motives. Research suggests that prevention-focused workers evaluate how desirable a position is in terms of the job security, physical working conditions, and earnings it offers. Promotion-focused workers, in contrast, are more concerned with the potential for self-growth, skill development, and challenge that a position affords.[4]

So if you want to know how someone is motivated, his or her occupation provides a valuable clue. But remember to look at not only the *kind* of career a person has chosen, but whether or not the person is actually *satisfied* with the choice. An accountant who constantly complains that his job doesn't give him enough freedom to express his true talents probably *isn't* as prevention-focused as his profession suggests.

Interestingly, just as the demands of a particular job can tell you something about the person who would choose it, the nature of a particular sport can tell you a lot about the person who plays it. Basketball and football players, for instance, are more promotion-focused, on average, than tennis players and gymnasts. Gymnastics is about flawless performances—points get *deducted* for mistakes.

Tennis players can gain a point by hitting a hard shot, but they also have to stay focused on avoiding faults—if you mess up, the other guy gets a point. A sport that requires precision and avoiding error is a natural draw for the prevention-minded.

Basketball and football, on the other hand, are about *accumulating* points—there is no limit to how many times you can score, and the general idea is to keep *advancing* down the court or field and going for gains. Making good defensive plays also matters, but you ultimately have to capitalize on your opponent's mistakes—you have to score after sacking the quarterback or stealing the basketball—in order to gain points and win the game. So this makes playing basketball and football a good fit for the promotion-minded.

There is even evidence that the *position* you play on a team says something about your dominant motivational focus, too. For example, within a soccer team, attackers (the ones who typically score) are more promotion-focused than defenders.[5]

## Clues from Behaviors, Choices, and Feelings

So far, the information we've given you couldn't help you figure out whether our MSC colleague Jon's dominant motivation would be different from Ray's. They are roughly the same age (about forty), and they have the same occupation (research psychologist). They were both born and raised in the northeastern United States. Where we can really begin to tell Jon and Ray apart is by looking at *how* they do what they do—their everyday behavior.

If you have the ability to observe your target audience in action (for instance, if it's your employee, your spouse, your child, or your student), you should have little difficulty determining whether they have a dominant promotion or prevention focus. Just look for these behavioral clues:

### Promotion-Focused People:

- **Work quickly.** They are eager to reach their goal *and* eager to move on to the next opportunity. This could result in the *quality* of their work suffering.
- **Consider lots of alternatives.** This makes them great brainstormers and creative problem solvers. It also makes them reluctant to commit to *one* way of doing things, which can lead to procrastination.
- **Are open to new opportunities.** Count on them to say yes to opportunities for gains, even risky ones. Being so open also results in their often getting overextended.
- **Have a rosy outlook.** They may be speedy, but they aren't necessarily good *judges* of time. Because their plans tend to be "best-case scenarios," they often underestimate how long tasks will take. (Their optimism applies to others' outcomes as well. They are the ones who will say, "Don't worry about it. You'll do great!")
- **Seek positive feedback, and lose steam without it.** Negativity and doubt are the enemies of promotion motivation. They'll look to you again and again for the praise that keeps them going.
- **Feel happy or sad.** Promotion-focused people feel joyful and confident when things are going well and feel sad and discouraged when they aren't. They cheer themselves up by imagining how much better things will be in the future. In the natural ups and downs of everyday life, they are the ones who see the glass half full.

**Prevention-Focused People:**

- **Work slowly and deliberately.** Attempts to get them to move it along will be either ignored or met with open hostility. They are interested in accuracy, not speed; quality, not quantity. They don't procrastinate and instead get started on time and do what's required of them.

- **Are prepared.** They've thought through all the options, imagined every kind of possible downside or disaster, and are "prepared for the worst." (It is the promotion-focused who "hope for the best.")

- **Are stressed by short deadlines.** Thinking through and preparing for all the things that could go wrong takes time. When there isn't *enough* time, prevention-minded people feel underprepared and are easily rattled.

- **Stick to known ways of doing things.** Tried-and-true methods are vastly preferred. If you want to do things in a new way, you'd better have darn good evidence that it works *and* it is necessary. Their motto is "If it ain't broke, don't fix it."

- **Are uncomfortable with praise or optimism.** *Visibly* uncomfortable. And even when faced with evidence that nothing can go wrong, they're never really relaxed until it's all over. They will shy away from their promotion-motivated friends prior to an important test or presentation in order to avoid hearing, "Don't worry about it. You'll do great!" That kind of "support" drains the vigilance they need to stay motivated.

- **Feel worried or relieved.** Prevention-motivated people, especially those who are successful, usually feel a little worried or apprehensive. Even when things are going well, they don't want to lose the vigilance that works for them. So they imagine what could go wrong if they aren't careful enough or work hard enough. After a big success they will feel relieved, and even content, for a while . . . but only a while. Soon they will be nervous again about what might happen if they let their guard down. They don't see the glass half empty but, instead, imagine it becoming empty if they are not vigilant enough.

## Clues from Values and Speech

*Better safe than sorry,* or *nothing ventured nothing gained?* The expressions we use in everyday conversation, the little nuggets of wisdom we impart to others offer a window into our dominant motivational focus.[6] Here are some popular proverbs that reveal a lot about the person who uses or agrees with them:

### Prevention Proverbs

*A bird in the hand is worth two in the bush.*
　　(translation: Avoid risk when things are satisfactory now)

*All that glitters is not gold.*
　　(translation: Don't make the mistake of being fooled by appearance.)

*Don't put all your eggs in one basket.*
　　(translation: Don't leave yourself vulnerable to disaster.)

*Don't count your chickens before they hatch.*
　　(translation: Don't be overconfident or overoptimistic.)

*Haste makes waste.*
> (translation: Don't rush. Be careful and thorough.)

## Promotion Proverbs

*It will be a piece of cake.*
> and (one of our favorites)

*A pessimist sees the difficulty in every opportunity; an optimist sees the opportunity in every difficulty.*
> (translation: Be optimistic!)

*Better late than never.*
> (translation: Don't worry about deadlines when there are things to enjoy or explore now. This one makes prevention-minded people shudder.)

*Go for broke.*
and
*Throw caution to the wind.*
and
*Go big or go home.*
> and (one of our favorites)

*A ship in the harbor is safe, but that is not what ships are built for.*
> (translation: It's worth taking a risk for a big gain.)

*To the victor go the spoils.*
> (translation: Gains come from winning.)

More generally, we can see evidence of promotion and prevention focus in the personal values people hold dear. Prevention-minded people are fond of tradition. They see conformity—the following of agreed-upon rules of conduct—as a good thing, and they put a premium on security (their own, their family's, and their community's). And, again, *if it ain't broke, don't fix it*. They resist change because it could make things worse. Only if they are in danger will they consider change. Change has to be a necessity for them to get on board with it.

Promotion-minded people place more value on advancing forward, self-direction, and novel experiences. (Did we mention *variety is the spice of life*? That's a promotion proverb, too.) They are open to change and ready to change quickly—if it offers new opportunities for gain. They know there's risk involved, but if there's a chance for real progress, they're willing to give the devil they don't know the benefit of the doubt.[7]

## Changing Focus, at Least Temporarily

Sometimes you don't just want to identify someone's focus—you want to *change* it. This occurs when the task at hand is best done in a particular focus, because the strengths of one focus (either promotion or prevention) are the best match with what the task demands. You don't want to just identify someone's focus and stick with it if it is the wrong focus for the current task or situation. Imagine, for example, that you need your employee to generate creative ideas, but you've noticed that he's about as cautious as the day is long, so he could probably use a little promotion focus to get the job done rather than staying in a prevention focus. You need your wide-eyed optimist of a spouse to start taking your finances and budgeting a lot more seriously, so a little more prevention focus is in order. Or maybe you've got a great prevention-focused product to sell (like insurance) to a group of people who think they are immortal (like young men).

The good news is, it turns out people can be fairly easily switched from one focus to the other, at least temporarily. And a temporary switch may be all that's needed for them to make a decision or complete a task with the optimal focus. You can also use these same techniques to change your *own* focus when you feel your dominant focus isn't working for you. The more you practice them, the more natural and automatic it will become to look at your world through a lens that's different from your usual one.

## What Will Happen If I Do This?

Perhaps the most straightforward way to shift your own or someone else's motivational focus is to think about what will happen from performing a particular act or making a particular choice—think about specific potential outcomes. To adopt a promotion focus, a person needs to concentrate on what there is to *gain* in a particular situation. In experiments, we've asked participants to think about what they can gain by choosing a mug or, alternatively, by choosing a pen (as an eager way to make a choice in a marketing study on preferences), or told them that they will get to do something fun—like play Wheel of Fortune—if they do well on a task, to effectively place them in a promotion focus.

So if your wife is trying to work up the courage to accept a new job offer, but she is a bit nervous about leaving her current job for something less familiar and therefore riskier, she should try focusing on the pay increase, the greater creative freedom, and the exciting opportunities the new job will provide. The more she deliberately thinks about the gains, the more promotion-focused she will become and the more comfortable she will be taking the leap into the unknown.

To adopt a prevention focus, on the other hand, a person needs to think about what might be lost by not taking some action or making some choice. We've given participants a prevention focus by asking them to think about what they would lose by not choosing the mug or, alternatively, by not choosing the pen (as a vigilant way of making a choice), or by telling them that they would have to do something tedious—like proofreading—if they didn't do well on a task. (We realize this doesn't sound fun, but we never promised you that prevention focus would be fun. Just, in its own way, very effective.)

Imagine, for example, that your husband has been procrastinating about doing home repairs and could use a little more prevention motivation to get himself going. He should stop thinking about all the great Sunday sports games he could watch and instead spend some time dwelling on what could go wrong if he doesn't get busy on the repairs. He needs to think about how the house will not maintain its current value, how water from the clogged gutters could be undermining your home's foundation, how you are wasting so much money heating areas that are poorly insulated. Next thing you know, he'll have his caulking gun in hand, vigilantly defending your homestead (and your wallet) from the winter chill.

## Make a List

Promotion focus can also be induced by asking people to list—or choose from a list—of positive things that could happen to them in a relevant context. For instance, you are more likely to be promotion-focused during vacation planning if you are asked to list all the wonderful things you'd like to do on your holiday (e.g., eat delicious meals, sleep in, enjoy a book on the beach). If, on the other hand, you list the negative things you want to actively avoid on your holiday (e.g., an expensive hotel bill, gastrointestinal issues) you are going to be a much more prevention-focused vacation planner.[8]

This is a strategy that one of us (Grant Halvorson) actually uses frequently to shift her own focus. She explains:

I am fairly promotion-focused when it comes to my work, but I have a tendency to be *all* prevention at home. Thanks to a combination of strict German upbringing and being a mother to two young children, I usually look at my personal life as a long series of duties and responsibilities. After my first child was born, I began to see danger lurking around every corner—the world was suddenly filled with germs, predators, and pointy objects—and it's been that way ever since. So enjoying things like a vacation abroad is difficult for me. (*How will the kids behave on the plane? Will they get jet lag? Will they need allergy medication? Will they be so bored they drive us crazy?*)

It got to the point where I was making it impossible for myself to just enjoy myself—what I needed, quite clearly, was to put my promotion hat back on. Now, when my husband and I consider taking a trip, I literally force myself to write a list of all the reasons that the trip will be wonderful—the things we will be able to see and do, the friends and family we'll get to spend time with. When I feel myself starting to fret again about jet lag and the availability of twenty-four-hour pharmacies, I read through the list, visualizing everything I have to *gain* by going on an adventure. Suddenly I am looking forward again to the trip and not worrying about whether everything will work out perfectly.

## Reflect on Your Future or Your Past

In recent years, the most common manipulation of motivational focus in the laboratory has been to ask participants to write brief essays (a paragraph or two) about either their hopes and aspirations (their promotion ideals) or their duties and obligations (their prevention oughts). When you write about (or simply think about) your dreams—like meeting Mr. or Ms. Right, having a vacation home in the Caribbean, or writing a prize-winning novel—you become more promotion-focused. When you write about your responsibilities—

like providing for your children, saving for retirement, or giving back to your community—you shift into a prevention focus.

This technique works equally well whether you are writing about your future (i.e., goals you intend to achieve) or your past (i.e., times when you have successfully achieved them). If you are someone who keeps a journal and you feel like you need a little more promotion or prevention in your life, you can easily incorporate a quick paragraph about either dreams or duties into your entries on a regular basis—over time, this will make shifting into the focus you want to adopt more automatic.

This is also a great technique for teachers to use in the classroom. When the subject matter requires a creative approach (for instance, in art, drama, or writing classes), having students think about their aspirations will bring about a creativity-friendly promotion focus. If, however, carefulness and accuracy are required (for example, in mathematics and science courses), having students think about responsibilities will induce a diligent prevention focus—and far fewer exploding test tubes in the chemistry lab.

## Put It in a Frame

One of the earliest methods of manipulating motivational focus that we developed is something called *task framing*. The basic idea is that you ask people to do exactly the same thing, like try to do their best on a set of puzzles, but you subtly vary what they think the point of doing well is. To put them in a promotion focus, you tell them that if they do well, they will gain something. If, for instance, you are paying them four dollars to be in your experiment, you inform them that they will gain an extra dollar if they do well. To put them into a prevention focus, you instead pay them five dollars to be in the experiment, but tell them that they will *lose* a dollar if they don't perform well. As we mentioned earlier in the book, the outcomes in this case are actually the *same*: performing well means ending with five dollars and not performing well means ending with four dollars. It's the different framing of these same outcomes that does the trick.

You can use this kind of framing with just about anything, just by tweaking the incentives. Kids who turn in their homework get to go on a field trip (promotion), or everyone gets to go on a field trip *except* kids who fail to turn in their homework (prevention). Employees get something special (pay; privileges) for hitting a performance target (promotion), or they lose the same benefit for coming in below that target (prevention). When performing to some criterion is thought of as attaining a gain, it creates a promotion focus. When failing to perform to the same criterion is thought of as failing to avoid a loss, it creates a prevention focus.

## Tap into a Different Self

As we mentioned earlier, people who see themselves as independent tend to be promotion-focused, while those who see themselves as interdependent are more prevention-focused. Given this, you can shift a person's sense of self—and consequently his or her dominant focus—in a variety of ways. When people work on projects individually they are more likely to feel independent (and more promotion-focused), but when they work in teams they feel (and are) interdependent (and more prevention-focused). In fact, simply viewing images of either individuals or groups (like a sports team or a family) can activate different self-views.[9]

For instance, people who saw an advertisement for a running shoe that contained images related to individual sports (marathon, swimming, golf, cycling) became more promotion-focused, and as a result preferred the version that claimed the shoe would "increase the power of running" over the one that claimed it would help them "avoid the pain of running." Those who instead saw an advertisement featuring team sports (football, basketball, baseball, soccer) became more prevention-focused and preferred the ad that touted avoiding pain to the one on increasing power.[10]

So if you want your employees, your students, or your customers to adopt a promotion mindset, keep the emphasis on the individual: *You* can reach this goal. *You* can master this material. *You* can benefit from this product. If, on the other hand, a prevention mindset is called for, talk about what they are doing in terms of the group: *We* can reach this goal *working together*. *We* can *all* master this material. *Your family* can benefit from this product. Shifting between "I" and "We" language and imagery is one of the easiest ways to create the shift in focus you are looking for.

## Models Matter

Is your mother a pillar of prevention motivation, always organized and in control and constantly warning you about the dangers lurking . . . well, basically everywhere? Is your brother a risk-taking, promotion-focused daredevil who once backpacked across Europe on a hundred dollars and a smile? If you are close to someone who has a strong motivational focus, studies show that simply *thinking about* that person is enough to shift your own focus in that direction.[11] And if you don't know someone personally who fits the bill, you might try thinking about a famous figure or role model who does.

### Famous Promotion-Focused Figures

Sir Richard Branson—founder of Virgin Records, Virgin Airlines, and Virgin Galactic, self-made billionaire, and holder of multiple world records for fastest journeys by air

Evel Knievel—daredevil motorcyclist and *Guinness Book of World Records* record holder for most broken bones survived in a lifetime

Muhammad Ali—world heavyweight champion, social activist, outspoken conscientious objector to the Vietnam War, and *Sports Illustrated* Sportsman of the Century; nicknamed "the Greatest"

### Famous Prevention-Focused Figures

Martha Stewart, author, designer, television personality, and self-described "maniacal perfectionist"

Fred Astaire—world-renowned dancer, choreographer, and actor, known particularly for his technical control, grace, precision, and relentless insistence on frequent rehearsals and retakes

Margaret Thatcher—longest-serving (and only female) British prime minister of the twentieth century and icon of Conservatives and Hawks; nicknamed "the Iron Lady"

## Mottoes Matter

Just as proverbs tell you something about the people who author and subsequently use them, slogans and mottoes can reveal a great deal about the groups or organizations they represent. For instance, the Medici family, the wealthy and powerful Florentine bankers who ruled much of Italy for nearly three centuries, had a particularly appropriate motto: "Money to get power, and power to guard the money." The U.S. Marine Corps motto, *Semper fidelis*, or "Always Faithful," is a reminder of their dedication to one another, to the corps, and to their country. The *New York Times's* motto, "All the News That's Fit to Print," was intended by founder Adolph S. Ochs to convey his commitment to reporting the news impartially. And Google's informal motto, "Don't Be Evil," is a reminder to the company's leaders and employees that they should not maximize short-term profits at the expense of the public good.

You can influence the *collective* motivational focus of your group, team, or organization through the mottoes you choose to represent your values and philosophy. Even though a team may start out with members with a variety of viewpoints, over time they tend to develop what psychologists call a *shared reality*, or an agreed-upon way of seeing and doing things, that is either promotion- or prevention-focused.[12]

Studies show that people become more promotion focused when they are told that the motto of the group they are joining is "If there is a will there is a way," but more prevention-focused when told the motto is "An ounce of prevention is worth a pound of cure."[13] So choosing the right slogan can be a powerful way to get your group on the same motivational page.

### Promotion-Focused Mottoes

*Fortune Favors the Bold* (in Latin: *Audentes fortuna juvat*)
—366th Fighter Wing

*Forward*
—Churchill College, Cambridge

*Faster, Higher, Stronger*
—Olympics

*Rethink Possible*
—AT&T

### Prevention-Focused Mottoes

*The Fruit of Learning Is Character and Righteous Conduct*
—University of Mumbai

*The Buck Stops Here*
 —Harry Truman

*Be Prepared*
 —Boy Scouts of America

*Never Again*
 —Jewish Defense League

In part 1 of *Focus*, you learned about the differences between having a promotion or a prevention motivational focus. You learned how our focus affects everything we are—what we pay attention to, what we remember, what we feel—and everything we do—how we work, love, parent, make decisions, and relate to other people. Understanding focus helps you to recognize your and other people's motivational strengths and weaknesses, and to know what will bring out the best in yourself and in others. You also learned how to "diagnose" promotion or prevention focus in yourself and in other people. And you learned how you can change someone's focus, including your own, should the need arise.

In part 2 we'll show you how to use all this knowledge to become an effective *influencer*. You'll be able to craft a message or frame a task in a way that inspires, engages, and persuades, by mastering the subtle art of speaking your audience's motivational language.

# PART TWO

# MOTIVATIONAL FIT

# CHAPTER 9

## It's the Fit That Counts

Our MSC colleagues Jon and Ray have a big deadline coming up. They are both applying for research grants from the National Science Foundation. The paperwork is so arduous, it makes filing one's income taxes seem like a stroll on the beach. Tackling such a complex, unpleasant job requires *lots* of motivation. This is not a case where a particular kind of motivation is a better match for the task (as we discussed in chapter 8). Either a promotion or a prevention focus will do. What does matter is that the motivation be strong. So what should we say to Jon and Ray to strengthen their motivation and get the job done? As you'll see in examples throughout the remaining chapters of this book, you can motivate someone— to perform better, to want a particular product, or to embrace an idea or belief—*much* more effectively if you tailor your message to fit his or her motivational focus. We already know that the encouragement that "fits" for Ray will not "fit" for Jon. But how do you create *fit*, exactly?

## Just Give Them What They Want?

The sense of "fit" that we are probably all most familiar with is a match between what someone wants or needs and what the person believes an idea, action, or product provides. (For Jon and Ray, applying for an NSF grant "fits" with their very real and pressing need for research funds.) Marketers, of course, tell stories in order to shape or influence those beliefs, to guide us toward their particular products. So yuppie liberals will want to drive a Prius because its story says "I'm smart and eco-conscious," and that's essentially what yuppie liberals want to be. Anxious parents will make their daughter's first car a Volvo because its story says "I put safety first when it comes to my child," which is precisely what they are looking to do.

But our research suggests that *motivational fit* is a subtler concept than just "give them what they want" or "match your product to their need." Put simply, motivational fit happens when you create a match not only between what people want and what they get, but also between what they want and *how* they go about getting it—*the way they reach their goals.*[1]

For example, you can lose weight by eating less *or* by exercising more. You can realize your retirement dreams by embracing risk *or* avoiding it like the plague. You can make a good impression by saying more *or* saying less. People definitely have preferences about the way they do things—about the *process*, not just the outcome—and those preferences are determined by their promotion or prevention motivation. We experience motivational fit when our current motivational focus is *sustained* or *supported* by the means we use—the *manner* of our decision making, the *kind* of information we consider, or the particular *strategy* we adopt to pursue a goal. So Jon needs to tackle his grant application in a way that sustains his prevention-focused motivation—maintaining or increasing his natural *vigilance*. Ray, on the other hand, needs an approach that will work with his promotion-focused motivation to enhance his natural *eagerness*.

Influencers are used to thinking a lot about what people want, but tend to overlook the fact that people also have preferences about the *way* they get it—and these preferences can be just as strong motivationally as their desire to fulfill the goals themselves. When they experience motivational fit, people tell us that they *feel right*, and they become more strongly engaged in what they are doing. Feeling right and having stronger engagement, in turn, lead to increases in perceived value.[2] If Jon and Ray experience fit, they will be more motivated to complete their applications on time—and because they'll be more engaged in the process, they'll value the grant-writing activity more and turn in superior work.

When people consider your product or idea and experience motivational fit, they feel more attracted to it, have more confidence in their feelings, and will pay more or do more for it.[3] They will trust your laundry detergent (or political candidate or sales campaign) to live up to its promise, compared to its competitors. When they experience fit when listening to how you describe a task, or when receiving your feedback, they will perceive it as more fair, they'll be more engaged, and they'll work more effectively.

As you'll see, the tailoring we are arguing for can be incredibly subtle. For instance, if you wanted to sell cars to Ray and Jon, you should talk to promotion-focused Ray about "better mileage" but describe it as "lower fuel costs" to prevention-focused Jon. You should draw Ray's attention to the "bonus" features he will get if he buys the Limited Edition (after all, he wants whatever is the latest and the best), but emphasize to Jon what a "mistake" he would be making if he *didn't* buy it (since he doesn't want the mistake of buying an inferior product). If you think these differences wouldn't matter much . . .

after all, it's just a difference in choice of words . . . you would be wrong.

What the customer ends up *getting* may be the same—Ray and Jon may in fact drive away in identical cars. But how they come to buy those cars—through the promotion-focused strategy of seizing opportunities to get something good (e.g., better mileage or bonus features) or the prevention-focused strategy of avoiding something bad (e.g., high fuel costs or an inferior product)—is motivational night and day. Knowing which version will be effective for your employee, child, student, or customer, for your particular message or product, is the key to creating fit.

In this chapter we'll describe the basics of creating motivational fit and show you how to predict when and why it will occur. Let's begin with one of our favorite examples of the power of fit—the marketing of the Riedel wineglass.

## If the Glass Fits, Drink with It

In his influential bestseller *All Marketers Are Liars*, Seth Godin describes how the success of Riedel is in the genius of its story, and how that story changes the experience of the consumer. In the end, it's a story about the vital importance of *means*.

The motivation behind drinking good wine is promotion-focused—it's about pleasure, sophistication, and status. No one ever shelled out a hundred dollars for a bottle of wine so that they would be *safer* when they drank it, or because it's a good value for the money. There is also some fairly compelling evidence showing that most people can't actually tell the difference in a blind taste test between inexpensive and expensive wines. But that doesn't stop (promotion-focused) people from *wanting* expensive wines, because deep down they still believe that good wine *should* and *will* cost more—that's what makes it a luxury—and thus they want to drink a more expensive wine. So pricing your wine at one hundred dollars a bottle instead of ten dollars is an example of taking into account people's beliefs, and matching a product to what people want.

The glass you drink that wine out of, on the other hand, is not as much about what you *want*, as it is about *how* you consume it. Drinking expensive wine out of a twenty-dollar Riedel glass *feels right*, because it seems like the right way to get a pricey, high-status wine from the bottle to your lips. Drinking from the *best* glass sustains the goal of tasting the *best* wine, which creates fit—fit that translates into making the whole tasting experience more worthwhile.

Indeed, wine connoisseurs swear that wine actually *tastes better* in a Riedel glass, despite the fact that scientifically conducted tests show no difference between a Riedel glass and its one-dollar equivalent. But as Godin points out, even if the difference between the glasses isn't real, the difference in reported value to the customer is real. What he and the people at Riedel may not realize, however, is that this is not just "cheap talk"—the actual experienced value of the wine *is* enhanced because of motivational fit.

## Feeling Fit

As we mentioned earlier, the essence of experiencing fit is being able to pursue one's goal in a way that *sustains* (rather than *disrupts*) promotion or prevention motivation. In other words, it's doing things the way you want to do them, given how you are motivated. *Eager* means (e.g., being bold and optimistic, being fast, taking chances) fit with promotion motivation. When you do things in a bold way, you are more likely to gain, and you don't close off opportunities to advance.

*Vigilant* means (e.g., being careful, being accurate, avoiding mistakes) are a good fit with prevention motivation. When you do things in a careful way, you are better at avoiding losses and are less likely to make mistakes.

When we ask people how fit feels—what kind of an experience it is—they reliably tell us that it just *feels right* to them. Feeling "right," incidentally, is not the same thing as having a "pleasant" feeling. Thinking everything is going to be sunshine and roses might feel *pleasant*, but to someone who is prevention-focused, thinking this way will also feel *wrong*, because it's dangerously naïve. On the other hand, methodically preparing for worst-case scenarios will feel right, despite the fact that thinking that way doesn't feel pleasant at all.

(One of the most irritating things that the prevention-focused have to put up with is being told that they must get pleasure from being the worrywart and sweating the details, since that's what they always do. To be clear—it does not give them pleasure, but it does feel like the *right* thing to do. And feeling right about it does matter, because by knowing that they have their bases covered, they can experience the satisfaction of being effective.)

## Two Paths to Persuasion

When people feel "right," they are more persuaded by your message—whether you are asking them to buy your toothpaste, do their homework, or accept the fact that their job description needs to change. But how exactly does "feeling right" translate into more effective persuasion? It turns out that motivational fit influences your attitude toward an idea or product through two different mechanisms, depending on the *importance* of the idea or product to you.

## When It Really Matters

When the message concerns something that *is* important—something that is highly relevant to you personally—feeling right from fit affects persuasion by *increasing your confidence in your own judgment*. In so doing, it intensifies your reaction (either more positive or more negative) to what you are seeing and hearing. So your initial feeling or opinion becomes even stronger. Feeling wrong from nonfit, on the other hand, weakens your reaction (either less positive or less negative).

So if you are a real automobile aficionado—someone truly passionate about cars—and you are thumbing through your monthly issue of *Motor Trend* magazine, you will probably pay particular attention to the car advertisements, forming opinions on each new model. If you also experience fit from the advertisement (say, because it is gain-framed and you are promotion-focused when it comes to cars), then you will feel right, and feel more confident in your judgments. If you like a particular new model, you will like it *even more* because of fit. If another one is a total turnoff—let's say you think it's too boxy and boring—it will be an even bigger turnoff because of your higher confidence from fit.

## When, Frankly, It Really Doesn't Matter

When the message concerns something that is *not* important or personally relevant to you, however, you don't even bother weighing the pros and cons to make a judgment. You don't care enough to engage in critical evaluation. *You just use the "feeling of rightness" itself as a guide*—if I feel right (from fit), then it must be a good thing. If I feel wrong (from nonfit), it must be bad.

So imagine you are *not* an automobile aficionado—you can't tell a

Porsche from a Pontiac—and you are thumbing through your Sunday newspaper. You probably won't pay particular attention to the car advertisements, though you may give them a cursory read. If you also experience fit from the advertisement (this time, say, because it is loss-framed and you are prevention-focused in general), then you will feel right—and that feeling of rightness will form the basis of your opinion about the car. If you feel right when looking at a picture of a Honda Accord, then you will feel favorable toward Accords. (If the advertisement creates nonfit, however, you'll feel wrong and be less favorable to Accords.)

Let's illustrate these two paths to persuasion again, this time with a research example. Participants were asked to look at a print ad that described the *negative* effects of drinking coffee on health. It included statements like "Coffee blocks the absorption of vitamin C," and "Love your body instead of your coffee. Reduce your caffeine intake." In one version of the experiment, they were also told that the ad was scheduled to appear in a national campaign the following month, and that the ad agency that created it would take their reaction to the ad very seriously.

Because their opinion was so important, it made the message personally relevant. As a result, all the readers paid close attention to the arguments in the ad. Since the message arguments advocated *against* coffee, this made their attitude toward coffee more negative. Those who experienced motivational fit while reading the message were significantly *more* negative about coffee than those who experienced nonfit. In other words, fit intensified their (negative) reaction to the subject of the (negative) ad. The (largely unconscious) thought process looks something like this:

**Reader Who Experiences Fit:** *After paying close attention to* *the arguments, I've formed an opinion about coffee—it's bad. I feel right about my opinion. Coffee must be really bad.*

**Reader Who Experiences Nonfit:** *After paying close attention to the arguments, I've formed an opinion about coffee—it's bad. But I don't really feel right about my opinion. Coffee must not be so bad.*

In another version of the experiment, people were given the same ad, but told that it was a *draft* of an ad that may or may not appear in *European* newspapers, possibly *the following year.* For this group, the ad wasn't particularly important or personally relevant, so there was no real need to pay close attention to the ad's arguments. Instead, the participants could just use their feelings of rightness (or wrongness) as their guide to their attitude about coffee. In this low-importance case, motivational fit resulted in *more* positive attitudes toward coffee, while nonfit produced more negative attitudes.[4] In this case, the thought process (also largely unconscious) looks something like this:

**Reader Who Experiences Fit:** *I don't really care much about all this information so I'm not going to pay much attention to it. But right now I'm feeling right about coffee. Coffee must be pretty good.*

**Reader Who Experiences Nonfit:** *I don't really care much about all this information so I'm not going to pay much attention to it. But right now I'm not feeling right about coffee. Coffee must not be so good.*

So what does this all mean for you, the persuader or motivator? How can you use this knowledge to be more effective with your audience—whether "your audience" is your employees, your students, supermarket shoppers, or your child? Well, in a nutshell, it means that delivering your message with motivational fit, all by itself, will make whatever you are advocating more appealing when the issue is *not* very important to your audience—when it's about something relatively trivial (e.g., which soda brand they buy), something they don't know much about (e.g., how Super PACs work), or something that affects only other people (e.g., foreign aid).

If, on the other hand, the issue *is* important to your audience, you will need to make sure your message not only fits your audience but also contains *strong arguments*; the strong arguments will persuade your audience to accept the message's conclusion, and then feeling right from motivational fit will make them more confident that they've drawn the correct conclusion. If instead you use poor, unconvincing arguments on an important issue for an audience in motivational fit, then your audience will feel right (i.e., confident) about *rejecting* your conclusion, and you will be worse off than before. So when the issue is not important you can take advantage of motivational fit even when your arguments are weak. But when the issue is important, you need to have solid, convincing arguments to take advantage of motivational fit.

## Do You Speak Fit? Oh, Yes, Fluently.

Most English-speaking people in America have no problem understanding the queen of England, Anthony Hopkins, or former *American Idol* host Simon Cowell. Despite their British accents, we have little difficulty grasping what they are saying. The same cannot be said for Ozzy Osbourne, the cast of the film *Trainspotting*, and half the character actors on *Masterpiece*. Their accents are just different enough from ours to make understanding their speech a challenge. Even though they are using the same language, the experience of the American listener is less *fluent*. In other words, it's more difficult to process.

The ads we use to sell products, and the feedback we use to motivate our employees, students, or children, can also differ in its fluency, or ease of processing. Research on fluency suggests that, in general, people like things more when they are easy to grasp quickly, and dislike them more when they are complex or somewhat contradictory. Perhaps this is why Ingmar Bergman's Swedish masterpiece *The Seventh Seal*, in which a medieval knight challenges Death to a game of chess, has fewer fans than Sylvester Stallone's *Rambo*.

As it happens, one way to enhance your message's fluency, and therefore its persuasiveness and likability, is to make sure it creates motivational fit. When ads for Welch's grape juice described the famous beverage as *energy-enhancing*, making it a promotion-focused product, buyers found the ad easier to process and rated the brand more positively when the ad message itself was also gain-framed,

*Get energized!*

rather than loss-framed,

*Don't miss out on getting energized!*

When Welch's grape juice was instead described as a source of antioxidants that *prevent cancer and heart disease*, making it a prevention-focused product, the ad message that was loss-framed,

*Don't miss out on preventing clogged arteries!*

was more fluent and more effective than the one that was gain-framed,

*Prevent clogged arteries!*[5]

So if you want to make sure your message is getting through—that it is easy to follow and fully understand—it pays to deliver it with motivational fit. People will "get" what you are saying and respond to it more strongly.

## We See What Fits (and That's About It)

When academics submit a paper to a journal for review, they get a response (many months later) that follows the same general format.

The journal editor begins by highlighting the paper's strongest qualities—what you did right. This is followed by a list of the paper's shortcomings—what you did wrong, or failed to do at all. Finally, there is a verdict—fix what's wrong and I'll publish it, or go back to the drawing board.

When you receive a response from an editor, the very first thing you do, no matter who you are, is skip to the end. The final verdict, after all, is what matters most. But which part would you read next—the praise or the criticism? If you are like Ray, you'll probably go back to the beginning to see what you did right and what the editor found promising—but if you are more like Jon, you'll dive right into the criticism and try to figure out where and how you could have gone wrong—to fix what you can and learn what to avoid next time.

In a way, people create their own motivational fit on a regular basis by paying particular attention to the aspects of feedback (or persuasive appeals, or products) that sustain their motivation.[6] In other words, you form your opinions, make choices, and take action based on the attributes that fit your focus, and you brush off or disregard the ones that don't.

For instance, promotion-focused shoppers are more likely to attend to descriptions of toothpaste that focus on what can be *gained*: teeth whitening, breath freshening, and enamel strengthening. The prevention-focused, on the other hand, are more sensitive to descriptions of how a toothpaste might help them *prevent* cavity, plaque, and gingivitis.

So if your message contains information that is about both gains *and* losses, pros *and* cons, or what went right *and* what went wrong—you can count on some selective tuning on the part of your audience. They are going to pay special attention to what fits and are more likely to disregard what doesn't.

Their greater engagement and attention will translate into better memory for that information, too.[7] If you want people to remember what you tell them, or to remember your product when choosing from a sea of alternatives, deliver your message with fit.

Incidentally, one way to remove the attention bias for information that fits is to convince your audience that the message is very important to them; people are more likely to pay attention to, and critically evaluate, all information when something really matters. (But then make sure you have strong arguments.)

## Fit Is Fair

One of the toughest things we ever have to do is tell people what they don't want to hear.

*No, you won't be getting a promotion at this time.*

*We aren't going to go on vacation this year.*

*You can't take my car on a road trip with your friends.*

*I know you already feel overworked, but here are three new projects you'll need to complete this quarter.*

*It's not you, it's me.*

There's no way to disguise the fact that bad news is bad news, so you can never hope to entirely remove its sting. But you can learn to deliver bad news in a way that softens the blow, by increasing the chances that it will be perceived as *fair*.

The key to making bad news seem fair is to match your delivery to the motivational style of the listener. For instance, imagine you are an executive who has to inform your employees about an upcoming companywide "reorganization"—news that is generally met with groans and dismay. You could choose to justify the reorganization using gain framing (e.g., the reorganization will "make the company more profitable"), which highlights the potential gains (sometimes called the "vision" speech). Or you could instead use loss framing (e.g., the reorganization will "prevent further financial losses"), which emphasizes the dangers avoided (sometimes called the "burning platform" speech).[8]

As you might expect, promotion- and prevention-minded employees judge bad news to be significantly more fair when its framing matches their focus. *Public* perceptions of a company's actions are also affected by fit: promotion-minded readers rated (real) layoffs at DaimlerChrysler as significantly more fair and reasonable when they were described as an opportunity to "promote market share," while prevention-minded readers took a more favorable view when the layoffs were justified as "preventing *loss* of market share."[9] (If their grant applications were—Heaven forbid—rejected, Ray would prefer to hear that the reviewers "did their best to accept just the very best proposals," while Jon would find it more fair if the reviewers "were careful to screen out all but the very best proposals." Neither, for the record, would be happy about it—but they'd be less likely to cry foul.)

How exactly does motivational fit increase fairness? Essentially it's because it decreases "could have" and "should have" thinking in the wake of bad news. When people experience unfavorable events, they engage in what psychologists call *counterfactual thinking*, or "what if" questioning, to decide if they were treated fairly.

"Could have" counterfactuals address questions like: Could things have turned out differently if the decision makers had taken another course of action? In other words, was it inevitable? Did my company have another option besides "reorganizing"? Could the reviewer have funded my research proposal?

"Should have" counterfactuals address questions like: *Should* the decision makers have taken the other course? In other words, did they knowingly do the wrong thing? Was it unethical? Are the top executives sacrificing lower-level jobs just to line their own pockets? Was my proposal rejected because the reviewer doesn't like me personally?

When "could have" and "should have" counterfactuals lead to "yes" answers, people are more likely to perceive their circumstances as unfair. But this is less likely to happen when people "feel right" about the message as a result of motivational fit; when there is fit, people feel less need to ask (and answer) these questions.

So the next time you find yourself having to take a project out of the hands of one team member who's clearly floundering and transfer it to another, you'll know whether to describe it as an "opportunity to devote your energy to other assignments" (for your promotion colleague) or as a way to "avoid being dangerously overloaded with work" (for your prevention colleague). And when giving the "it's not you, it's me" speech, you'll know whether to talk about "freeing you to find happiness elsewhere" (for your promotion ex-partner) or "not wasting any more of your time" (for your prevention ex-partner).

In this chapter, you've learned that when you experience fit, you feel right, you become more strongly engaged, and information is easier to process and remember. Feedback feels fair, and performance is enhanced. And this is only the beginning. Now that you understand *how* it works, you are ready to see what it can do for you.

In chapters 10–12, we'll take a closer look at how motivational fit shapes consumer preferences (and the price they're willing to pay) for everything from sunscreen to coffee mugs to health insurance. You'll see how it affects performance on basketball courts, in office cubicles, and in math classes, and how it helps people to manage their illness, work out regularly at the gym, pay their taxes, and fight teen smoking. And all of this can be accomplished simply by saying things just a *little* bit differently to different people.

# CHAPTER 10

# The Triumph of the Fittest

ONE OF THE KEY BENEFITS OF SHAPING A MESSAGE TO FIT WITH your audience's promotion or prevention focus is the enhanced motivation it creates. Experiencing fit really gets your juices flowing. Experiencing nonfit, on the other hand, disrupts motivation. When the instructions or feedback we hear doesn't gel with our dominant focus, it feels wrong, weakening engagement in our goal pursuit. In this chapter, we'll share with you some of our favorite examples of how the right motivational message can spell the difference between success and failure.

## Inspirational Role Model or Cautionary Tale?

Take, for instance, one of the most common ways we use to motivate young people: using the personal experiences of others as examples—in the form of either an *inspirational role model* (someone you aspire to be like) or a *cautionary tale* (someone whose path you wish to avoid). Which is more effective? Well, that depends (not surprisingly at this point) on whether the young person in question is promotion or prevention-minded.

If you are an educator or parent, you might find it useful to know that college students who are promotion-focused are more motivated to study when they hear about an alumnus whose postgraduate years have been a big success—the guy with the great job, a sense of purpose, and a sunny outlook for the future (i.e., the inspirational role model):

> I just found out I won a major scholarship for postgraduate study. Two major companies have also contacted me about great positions. . . . Right now, I'm extremely happy with my life. I feel like I know where I'm going and what I want. I never imagined that my future could be so amazing!

Prevention-focused students, on the other hand, study harder and procrastinate less when you frighten them with the tale of the aimless, jobless graduate, dwelling in darkness in his parents' basement, whose prospects aren't looking too good (i.e., the cautionary tale):

> I haven't been able to find a good job. I have spent a lot of time working in fast-food places, and doing some pretty boring stuff. . . . Right now I'm pretty down about things. I'm not sure where I'm going to go from here—I can't afford to go back to school, but I also can't find a good job. This is not where I expected to be at this point in my life![1]

If you are a health professional, or have a loved one who suffers from a treatable ailment, you'll be interested to know that promotion-focused diabetic patients are more likely to manage their diabetes effectively after learning about a fellow patient who exercises regularly, eats a healthier diet, and takes insulin as needed (an inspirational role model):

> When I was told I had diabetes, I was very frightened. Controlling my diabetes did not go very well in the initial period, but I'm doing much better nowadays. I have succeeded in adjusting my life to the diabetes. Every day I cycle to my work, and I exercise twice a week, which has a beneficial effect on my blood sugar levels. My diet is also properly adjusted to the diabetes. I eat much healthier and I have lowered my fat consumption. I eat many more vegetables and fruit now. In the beginning I found it difficult to take into account that I had to inject insulin, but now I am used to it. I think I handle my diabetes very well, especially because I know a lot about diabetes and because I engage in healthy behaviors. My blood sugar levels have been quite stable and low for years now, and I still don't suffer from any complications. According to my doctor, I should be able to maintain good health if I keep up the good work.

Prevention-focused patients, on the other hand, are more motivated after hearing about someone who has *not* adjusted well to life with diabetes and has *not* made the changes they know they have to make (a cautionary tale):[2]

> When I was told I had diabetes, I was very frightened. Controlling my diabetes did not go very well in the initial period, and it is still not going well. I have not succeeded in adjusting my life to the diabetes. I intended to cycle to my work every day, and I should exercise twice a week, because this would have a beneficial effect on my blood sugar levels. However, I have not put these intentions into practice yet. My diet is also not properly adjusted

to the diabetes. I love snack food and I am not so crazy about vegetables and fruit. I still find it difficult to take into account that I need to inject insulin; I can't get used to it. I don't think I handle my diabetes well, because of my insufficient knowledge of diabetes and because I engage in unhealthy behaviors. My blood sugar levels have been too high for years now, and I am beginning to develop some complications. According to my doctor, there is a very high chance that my health will deteriorate if I do not change my lifestyle.

## Doing It Their Way

You can also enhance someone's motivation by allowing them to work the way they want to—to do what comes naturally. (Unless, of course, what comes naturally is *not* working at all.) When we work with a strongly promotion-focused colleague, like Ray, we know that he's going to want to work quickly and creatively, take risks, and try lots of alternatives before settling on a final strategy. Practically speaking, this means that he will propose many potential answers to a given motivational question and that he will want to get into the idea-testing phase as soon as he can. Mistakes will be made that might have been avoided if there were a little less rushing, and he might occasionally get distracted by other sideline projects, but trying to make Ray work any other way (which some have tried) will leave him feeling stifled, unenthused, and far less effective.

Prevention-focused people, like our colleague Jon, instead need time to work deliberately and consider things thoroughly. If you want to collaborate with him, you must learn to tolerate the fact that he is going to be a little skeptical of whatever it is you are doing, and you'll need to be willing to get an early start on a big project—like applying for a grant. Prevention motivation makes it natural to want to avoid things, like mistakes, pitfalls, and tardiness—avoiding things that could undermine performance feels *right*. So much so, in fact, that people like Jon who are prevention-focused sometimes perform better *with* distractions and obstacles than without them.

For instance, in one study conducted by our MSC colleagues Tony Freitas and Nira Liberman, students were instructed to complete a set of math problems on a computer screen. For some of the students, humorous and highly distracting videos played on a portion of the screen, and the students were instructed to try to ignore the videos and focus on the math problems. There were, as you might expect, no differences between promotion-focused and prevention-focused students in math performance when there were no videos playing in the background. But when the distracting videos were playing, the differences were dramatic: promotion-focused students, not surprisingly, performed about 10 percent worse because of the distraction, while prevention-focused students (who have a lot more practice vigilantly *avoiding* things) performed 10 percent better! Not only did they solve more problems correctly, but they actually enjoyed solving them much more. So people perform better when they work on tasks whose demands provide a fit to their motivational focus—even when the demands make the task more difficult objectively.[3]

## Choosing Incentives

In the wake of the Gulf of Mexico oil spill and the public relations disaster it created for BP, BP's new CEO, Bob Dudley, made the somewhat surprising move in 2010 to change the rules governing employee bonuses. In an e-mail sent to all BP employees, he announced that *increasing safety* would be the sole criterion upon which bonuses would be calculated.

Mr. Dudley said the objective was "to ensure that a low-probability, high-impact incident such as the Deepwater Horizon tragedy never happens again." The key to achieving that goal, he said, is "the rigorous identification and management of every risk we face."

"We're determined to leave no stone unturned in the pursuit of our focus on safety," added spokesman Andrew Gowers.[4]

Many observers argued that this was merely another public relations maneuver, designed to give the impression (and really nothing more) that BP was developing a culture of safety. But let's assume for a moment that Bob Dudley was in earnest, and that he was genuinely trying to find an effective way to motivate his people to make safety their top priority. Is this the best way to get that particular job done—by awarding *bonuses* for safety?

One well-known problem with this approach is that it can end up incentivizing underreporting of safety problems rather than actually increasing safety. But a second important flaw is probably jumping right out at you—rewarding people for safety is a motivational *nonfit*. The thought of a bonus to be gained makes people eager and willing to take chances, which is the opposite of being vigilant and emphasizing safety. It's the thought of potential danger and loss that keeps people vigilant, not the thought of fatter paychecks. Penalties for *not* meeting new safety standards, on the other hand, would provide the kind of motivational fit that gets people working harder on safety.

So it's not as simple as "rewards are motivating." Choosing the incentive that will sustain or enhance the *right* motivation is essential. For another example, let's take a look at how creating motivational fit with different incentives changes the effectiveness of that ubiquitous marketing tool: the loyalty program.

Loyalty programs offer rewards, discounts, or other advantages to customers to keep them coming back. They usually involve a card that keeps track of your purchases or visits—once you've bought nine coffees you get your tenth one free, or perhaps one hundred dollars in purchases earns you one dollar cash back. If you're like us, your wallet is probably bursting with these things—some that get used fairly regularly and some that lie hidden behind your AAA card, remaining there long after the soup shops and video rental stores that issued them have gone out of business.

Since there are many different ways to structure a loyalty program, it pays to know *in advance* which will provide the right kind of incentive for your consumers and actually keep them coming back. The answer will depend, in part, on whether your description of the program provides motivational fit.

In one study, people who joined a gym with a $45-per-month membership fee were offered a loyalty program, which was presented in either a promotion- or a prevention-focused way:

With the *promotion* loyalty program, they would receive *money back* if they exercised at least eight times in the next four weeks.

This information was either framed in terms of *gain*:

*If you do, you will get $10 of your $45 monthly fee back* (language that fits for promotion ☺).

Or framed in terms of *loss*:

*If you don't, you won't get $10 back* (language that's a nonfit for promotion ☹).

With the *prevention* loyalty program, people paid only $35 up front and were told that they would have to pay a $10 *penalty* if they came in fewer than eight times in the next four weeks.

This information was either *gain* framed:

*If you do, you won't have to pay the $10 penalty* (language that's a nonfit for prevention ☹).

Or *loss* framed:

*If you don't, you will have to pay the $10 penalty* (language that fits for prevention ☺).

The descriptions that produced motivational fit (i.e., promotion + gain language, prevention + loss language) made the loyalty program seem much more valuable to members, and they reported significantly stronger intentions to exercise. Not surprisingly, this led to more frequent visits to the gym. Intriguingly, fit also resulted in higher-*intensity* workouts—so when you feel right and are more engaged because of fit, you also kick it up a notch.[5]

If you are creating a loyalty program, which description should you choose? Both of the descriptions that created *fit* worked equally well in the case of the gym membership, so if you don't have a strongly promotion- or prevention-focused consumer or product, you can go with either one. If, on the other hand, your audience or business is driven by one particular motivational focus, choose the description that provides the most fit with it.

But before ending this section on incentives, we need to emphasize that penalties are not the only way to create motivational fit for prevention. Rewards can also fit prevention *if they are set up properly*. Consider again the reward program to motivate better safety. Since safety is a prevention issue, you are going to want to use an incentive that fits with prevention. (Even if your employees are more promotion-focused in general, the activity you care about is prevention-focused, so that's what needs to be properly motivated.) The trick is not to make the reward program sound like the participants are starting at "0" and need to get better at safety during the year to end up attaining the "+1" reward. This is a fit for promotion, but not prevention motivation. Instead, the reward program needs to sound like the participants begin the year with the reward set aside for them (the reward is the status quo "0"), and they need to be better at safety during the year or they will lose the reward and end the year at "–1." This is a fit for prevention motivation.[6]

## Fit Helps You Get It Done

Imagine that you are a player in a regional league of the German Football Association, and you are about to practice penalty-shot kicking with your teammates and coach. (FYI: Playing in a regional league in Germany is a very big deal. Germans are *especially* serious about soccer, which is saying something.)

Before you take your first penalty kick, your coach approaches you and says (in German) one of the following things:

*You are going to shoot five penalties. Your aspiration is to score at least three times.*

or

*You are going to shoot five penalties. Your obligation is to not miss more than two times.*

Most players and coaches (and people, for that matter) wouldn't consciously note a difference. Either way, your goal is to score three or more times out of five. Moreover, you wouldn't expect a difference in wording to change performance for *these* players, who are all highly practiced in kicking penalty shots *and* highly motivated to perform at their best. But motivationally there is a *big* difference—the kind of difference that can mean winning or losing the game. Players in this study (which really was conducted with German semipro soccer players) performed significantly better when the framing of the instructions matched their dominant motivational focus. This was especially true for prevention-minded players, who scored nearly *twice* as many times when they received the "don't miss" instructions that created motivational fit.[7]

These researchers found the same patterns of results in the United States with college basketball players practicing three-point shots, who were instructed either to hit three or more out of ten, or not to miss more than seven. Prevention-focused players scored roughly twice as many times when they received matching feedback, and promotion-focused players scored about 30 percent more often. Once again, differences this big could win championships.[8]

You don't have to be an athlete to benefit from motivational fit—in fact, it's often the nonathletes we are most worried about, since they are the ones least likely to get the amount of exercise they need to stay healthy. Which of the following arguments about the importance of exercise do you find more compelling?

*Scientists say to accumulate physical activity throughout the day to stay healthy or improve your health.*

or

*Scientists say failing to accumulate enough physical activity throughout the day can lead to poor health.*

The phrasing matters, because when the importance of exercise is described in a way that provides motivational fit (the first one above being a fit for promotion and the second for prevention), people *double* (on average) their physical activity over the course of the following week![9]

Of course, being healthy is about more than just exercise—it's about eating right, too. Reasonable people can and do disagree about what the "optimal" human diet looks like, but almost everyone agrees that diets rich in fruits and vegetables have enormous health benefits. If only motivational fit could help us here, too. Oh, wait . . . it can! In a study we conducted with MSC colleague Scott Spiegel, we asked undergraduates—a group of people hardly known for their good eating habits—to keep a daily food diary for a week. Next, we gave them a pamphlet describing why they should eat more fruits and vegetables, and the pamphlets varied as to whether the reasons were promotion-focused (e.g., increased energy, attractiveness, good mood) or prevention-focused (e.g., boosting immune system, fighting disease). In this way, we were able to manipulate the students' motivation directly, making them (at least temporarily) promotion- or prevention-minded.

### Promotion-Focused Pamphlet

A diet rich in essential nutrients, like those found in fruits and vegetables, has direct effects on the biochemistry of the brain, resulting in increased energy, better moods, and a general sense of happiness and fulfillment. People who eat a balanced diet, of which fruits and vegetables are an integral part, can experience greater confidence and optimism, which in turn makes them more appealing to others as well as successful in their endeavors. Having an adequate supply of nutrients in the bloodstream is also important for maintaining attractive hair and skin and promotes an active metabolism, which burns fat and contributes to an over-all toned and attractive body. The vitamins and minerals found in fruits and vegetables provide the nourishment necessary for greater concentration and attentiveness and for maximizing men-tal abilities and creativity. Good nutrition can have a substantial positive effect on test performance and IQ (intelligence) scoring. If you eat the right amount of fruits and vegetables daily, you can experience an overall sense of feeling good about yourself.

### Prevention-Focused Pamphlet

Human beings require a whole regimen of nutrients for basic good health. Eating fruits and vegetables supplies the body with the nutrients it needs, enabling the body to produce substances from within which buffer it from the physical demands of the world we live in (pollution, daily stress, bad weather, etc.). The vitamins and minerals found in fruits and vegetables are known to play a protective role and help to repair already damaged tissues. Eating fruits and vegetables helps to facilitate the actions of the immune system, which works to keep you healthy and safe from illness. A well-nourished immune system stops pathogens (poisons) and neutralizes their toxins and forms a barrier against invading bacteria to prevent their spread. Certain vegetables have even been shown to be effective in protecting the body from cancer and heart disease. The nutrients found in fruits and vegetables also contribute to healthy teeth, gums, and bones. If you eat the right amount of fruits and vegetables, you can actively help keep yourself safe from illness and obtain overall good health.

There were actually two versions of each of these pamphlets—one that emphasized the benefits students could obtain by eating fruits and vegetables (gain framing) and one that emphasized the costs of *not* eating fruits and vegetables (loss framing).

**Promotion-Focused/Benefits Version**
If you eat the right amount of fruits and vegetables daily, you can experience an overall sense of feeling good about yourself.

**Promotion-Focused/Costs Version**
If you do not eat the right amount of fruits and vegetables, you cannot experience an overall sense of feeling good about yourself.

**Prevention-Focused/Benefits Version**
If you eat the right amount of fruits and vegetables, you can actively help keep yourself safe from illness and obtain overall good health.

**Prevention-Focused/Costs Version**
If you do not eat the right amount of fruits and vegetables, you cannot actively help keep yourself safe from illness and facilitate overall good health.

After reading the pamphlets, the students kept up their food diaries for another week. We then calculated the increase in servings of fruits and vegetables they consumed and found that, while all the versions were effective to some extent, the arguments that were delivered using language that created motivational fit (i.e., promotion/benefits and prevention/costs) were significantly more effective. Students who experienced fit ate 21 percent more servings of fruits and vegetables than those who experienced nonfit.[10]

In a second study, we tried to use motivational fit to influence performance in a context near and dear to our own hearts: to get undergraduates to turn in an essay *on time*. Participants in the study were told that they would be paid seven dollars for writing up and mailing via campus mail (or delivering by hand) a description of how they spent their upcoming Saturday. (It was to be written either Saturday evening or sometime on Sunday.) Before leaving the lab, we asked them to make a plan, detailing where, when, and how they would write the report. One version of the plan instructions was crafted in the language of promotion motivation:

WHEN: *imagine a good, convenient time when you will be able to write your report*

WHERE: *imagine a comfortable, quiet place where you might write your report*

HOW: *imagine yourself capturing as many details as you can and making your report vivid and interesting*

The other version of the plan instructions was crafted instead in the language of prevention motivation:

WHEN: *imagine times that will be bad or inconvenient for writing your report, so you can avoid these times*

WHERE: *imagine places that will be uncomfortable or have lots of distraction, so you can avoid writing your report in these places*

HOW: *imagine yourself not forgetting to leave any details out, and being careful not to make your report bland or boring*

Impressively, we found that when the planning instructions were delivered in the language that fit with a student's dominant motivational focus, they were more than 50 percent more likely to actually turn it in.[11] (Teachers and managers rejoice! The end to all those late or unfinished assignments is at hand! Children are usually more promotion-focused, so the promotion language will usually provide the best fit for them. Employees, on the other hand, can be given instructions tailored to their dominant motivation—assuming that, as their supervisor, you have some sense of what that is.)

It seems that no matter what the challenge, if you want people to tackle it more effectively and with greater intensity, you'll get a lot of mileage from describing the challenge using language that creates a good motivational fit.

## Enjoying Getting It Done

Fit can also be used to make work enjoyable. It is not just the inherent nature of a task—what you have to do in order to carry it out and complete it—that determines how much you enjoy doing it. How much you enjoy doing a task also depends on whether you experience motivational fit while you're doing it. What Ray and Jon need to do in order to balance their checkbook is the same, but carefully checking each entry, one after another, makes Ray groan and makes Jon smile.

The impact of fit on task enjoyment was demonstrated in one of the earliest MSC "fit" studies.[12] When the participants arrived at the study they were experimentally put into either a promotion state or a prevention state by asking them to describe either their hopes and aspirations in life or their duties and obligations in life, respectively. Then, as part of an "unrelated study," they were told that their task was to find as many four-sided objects as possible among dozens of multisided objects on a sheet of paper. They were told to act like scientists and treat the four-sided objects as organic material they needed to find, because they were either "helpful" proteins or "harmful" proteins.

What varied was how the manner of their search was framed. Half of the participants were told that "the way to do well on the task was to be eager and to try to maximize the helpful four-sided objects." The other half were told that "the way to do well on the task was to be vigilant and to try to eliminate the harmful four-sided objects."

Independent of their actual success in finding the four-sided objects, the participants enjoyed the task more when they experienced fit while doing it (the promotion participants trying to maximize, and the prevention participants trying to eliminate).

## SEEKING: A *Feel Right* Leader for a Lasting, Fit-Filled Work Relationship

Whether or not you consciously realize it, you want a leader who helps you reach your goals *in a way* that fits with *your* motivation. We all do. So which kind of leader is a good fit for each motivational focus?

Promotion-minded employees thrive under *transformational leaders*. A transformational leader is all about working toward ideals, supporting creative solutions, having long-term vision, and shaking things up (think Google or Pixar). *Transactional leaders*, on the other hand, emphasize rules and standards, protect the status quo, tend to micromanage, discourage errors, and focus more on effectively reaching more immediate goals (think the U.S. military). They run a tight ship—the kind of place in which a prevention-minded employee feels right at home.

When people find themselves working for a leader that fits, they say that they value their work significantly more and are less likely to want to leave their organization.[13] That means greater loyalty and productivity and far less employee turnover—good news for any company's bottom line.

Managers can create a good fit for their employees not only through their leadership style, but through the kind of feedback they deliver. When workers have a dominant promotion focus or are seeking advancement, they tend to increase effort when a supervisor offers them praise for excellent work. When, instead, they have a dominant prevention focus or are concerned primarily with job security, they are more likely to increase effort in the wake of criticism rather than praise. Please note that we are not saying that you should make up reasons to praise or criticize your employees—feedback should always be honest. We are simply pointing out that sometimes a different *emphasis* may be called for if you want to maximize motivation.[14]

There will be times, of course, when you either don't know the dominant focus of the person or group you are trying to motivate (or persuade), or you are trying to influence a group containing individuals with different motivations. When this is the case, which technique should you use? The good news is, you can often effectively use a mix of promotion and prevention approaches at the same time—for instance, offering bonuses for people who perform in the top 25 percent *and* creating penalties for those who perform in the bottom 25 percent. Research suggests that people will selectively tune in to the parts of your message that provide a good fit for *them*, while mostly tuning out the parts that create nonfit. So when in doubt, offer instructions, incentives, role models, and feedback that contain elements that fit with *both* motivations—this may be less effective than a perfectly targeted approach, but it will be much more effective than a message that provides no fit at all.

# CHAPTER 11

# Under the Influence

IN HIS CRITICALLY ACCLAIMED BESTSELLER *INFLUENCE*, PSYCHOLO-gist and world-renowned persuasion expert Robert Cialdini identifies six weapons of influence in the battle to direct human behavior:

1. *Reciprocation.* People feel obligated to "return the favor" when you do something for them. This is why so many of the fund-raising appeals you get in the mail contain things like free pencils or address labels.
2. *Commitment and consistency.* People feel obligated to do things they have publicly committed to doing, and they want to seem consistent—both to others and to themselves.
3. *Social proof.* People are more likely to do something if they see other people doing it.
4. *Liking.* People are more likely to be persuaded by you if they like you.
5. *Authority.* People are also more likely to be persuaded by you if you are a legitimate expert or authority figure.
6. *Scarcity.* People see (positive) things that are scarce or rare as more valuable. Which is why so many commercials tell you to

"act now" and buy those Civil War commemorative coins because inventory is "going fast."

In the nearly thirty years since *Influence* was first published, these principles have become *the* established tools of marketers, business leaders, politicians, diplomats, and activists to change the hearts and minds of people around the world. To Cialdini's collection of weapons, we offer a seventh: *motivational fit*.

Our studies show that when you use the right style of message, the recipient—whether it's a family member, a student in your class, a colleague at work, or a constituent in your congressional district—will find it more believable, trust it (and you) more, and pay more attention to it. That powerful combination results in far more effective persuasion. As the examples in this chapter will show, you can do extraordinary things—like getting teens to take their health seriously or getting potential tax cheats to actually pay up—if you deliver your appeal in a way that syncs with their motivational focus.

## Fight Teen Smoking

One of our favorite examples of the persuasive power of motivational fit comes from a study of antismoking ads aimed at teens. Rather than focusing directly on the effects of smoking on physical health, these ads highlighted smoking's *social* consequences—how you might be rejected by others as a consequence of your smoking habit (creating prevention motivation) or accepted as a consequence of being a nonsmoker (creating promotion motivation). Each version of the ad was also delivered in terms of either benefits or costs:

### Promotion Message + Benefits Frame (Fit ☺): Get Social Approval

*Images:* A teenager sitting among a group of other teens at a party puts out a cigarette, and his peers look at him approvingly. They smile and laugh together—one person gives him a high-five.

    *Caption:* "Don't smoke. Have a good time."

### Promotion Message + Costs Frame (Nonfit ☹): Miss Out on Social Approval

*Images:* Peers are looking at a teen approvingly, smiling and laughing. Then the teen starts smoking, and the friends turn their backs and start ignoring him.

    *Caption:* "Don't smoke. Smoking spoils a good time."

### Prevention Message + Benefits Frame (Nonfit ☹): Avoid Social Disapproval

*Images:* A teen is smoking at a party, and he's getting strongly disapproving looks from the others around him. He notices and stops smoking, and his peers stop looking irritated.

    *Caption:* "Don't smoke. Avoid being annoying."

### Prevention Message + Costs Frame (Fit ☺): Incur Social Disapproval

*Images:* A group of teens are standing around talking at a party. One teen starts smoking and gets strongly disapproving and irritated looks from those around him.

    *Caption:* "Don't smoke. Smoking is annoying."

Most people would look at these four sets of ads and see no real differences—the message seems more or less the same: *nonsmoking is better for relationships than smoking*. Nonsmokers are popular and have friends, and smokers are shunned. But in each version the message is experienced a little bit differently. In fact, the versions that created an experience of motivational fit (i.e., the promotion-focused/benefits and prevention-focused/costs combinations) were significantly more effective in increasing teen viewers' intentions to not smoke.

And that's not all. Teens who had a dominant promotion focus had particularly strong intentions not to smoke after seeing the promotion/benefits ad ("Don't smoke. Have a good time"), while prevention-focused teens (yes, they exist) had especially strong intentions not to smoke after seeing the prevention/costs ad ("Don't smoke. Smoking is annoying").[1] So for these particular viewers, there were *two* sources of motivational fit: (1) the fit between the focus and the delivery within the message itself and (2) the fit between their own dominant focus and the focus/delivery of the message. The more sources of fit you can create, the more persuasive your message will be.

Now think about the last time you tried to persuade someone— perhaps your spouse, your child, or a good friend—to avoid a dangerous behavior like smoking (or excessive drinking, or texting while driving). What did you say? There's a roughly 50 percent chance that you phrased your plea in a way that didn't provide fit. You might have told your spouse that you wanted him to quit smoking *so he wouldn't get cancer* (prevention/benefits framing) when it would have been more persuasive to tell him that if he keeps smoking, the odds are good that he *will* get cancer (prevention/costs framing). You might have told your teenager that *nobody likes or respects you* when you drink too much (promotion/costs framing)—when it would have been more persuasive to tell him that people will like you and respect you *more* when you keep your wits about you (promotion/benefits framing).

The good news is, you can be much more persuasive from now

on, and encourage the people you care about to live healthier, happier lives, if you take a moment to consider how to deliver your message with maximum fit.

## Fit Is Good for Your Health

These antismoking ads were effective not only because they created fit, but also because they found a way to cleverly get around the "smoking is bad for your health" approach—one that doesn't usually gel with young people—by making smoking about popularity and social isolation rather than lung cancer and heart disease. But there are circumstances in which we really do want kids to think about their physical well-being, too. So how can we get young people to pay attention to significant threats to their health and persuade them to take action to protect themselves? Part of the problem, of course, lies in the fact that young people often don't perceive themselves to be at risk in the first place. But the good news is that once you understand how promotion, prevention, and motivational fit work, you realize that different kinds of health messages will be effective, depending on your audience's perceived risk.

This was nicely demonstrated in a study conducted by market researchers Jennifer Aaker and Angela Lee, who used motivational fit to create advertisements aimed at college students for a product used to prevent and treat mononucleosis (or "mono," as it is often called).[2] They began by giving all the students in their study the following information:

Mononucleosis is so common that by the age of 40 over 85 percent of all individuals have already had the illness! This may seem hard to believe, especially to those who cannot ever imagine having had a mono-like illness. Because most people who contract mono have such a mild case, they never realize that a past scratchy sore throat or an unusual bout of fatigue was actually mono. Although anyone can contract the illness, the disease is most commonly seen by physicians in young adults between the ages of 15 and 30, especially those living in close contact to schools, colleges, and military bases. Mono can occur year-round, but most cases develop in the early spring.

Next, they manipulated the perceived risk for contracting mononucleosis, by telling some of the students that they could contract mononucleosis from common behaviors that they frequently engaged in (high risk), while telling others that mononucleosis is only spread through more unusual, rare behaviors (low risk).

## High Risk (More Prevention-Focused) Message

Participants in the high-perceived-risk condition read that they would be at risk for contracting mono if they "kissed, shared a toothbrush, shared a razor, had sex without a condom, engaged in oral sex; shared bottles of water or soda, or got a manicure." Since these are activities that undergrads often engage in, the message conveyed was that it is *very* easy for your typical college student to get mono.

## Low Risk (More Promotion-Focused) Message

Those in the low-perceived-risk condition read that they would only be at risk if they "got a tattoo, used needles, pierced body parts such as nipples, nose, tongue or belly button, were accidentally jabbed by a needle, had multiple sex partners during the same time period, were subject to the use of unsterilized equipment in a doctor's office, or had a blood transfusion." These are all relatively rare activities among college students, so the message conveyed was that your typical undergrad will *not* catch mono.

Finally, they read an advertisement for a real product (Supranox), described as an all-natural supplement that fights mononucleosis. The arguments in the ad were delivered with either a gain or a loss framing.

### Gain Framing

*Enjoy life! Know that you are risk free from mononucleosis. Let SUPRANOX™ be a part of your daily routine.*

*It is important to enjoy life. SUPRANOX™ helps you do that— by allowing you to fight an illness even before you have it. Enjoy Life. SUPRANOX™.*

### Loss Framing

*Don't miss out on enjoying life! Not knowing that you are risk free from mononucleosis. Let SUPRANOX™ be a part of your daily routine.*

*It is important not to miss out on enjoying life. SUPRA-NOX™ helps you do that—by allowing you to fight an illness even before you have it. Don't Miss Out on Enjoying Life. SUPRANOX™.*

Aaker and Lee found that students who perceived themselves to be at high risk became more prevention-focused and were more persuaded to try Supranox by the loss-framed version of the ad. Students who thought they had relatively low risk of contracting mono (which is generally the normal attitude for most young people with respect to any illness or disease) were more promotion-focused, and as a result were more persuaded by the gain-framed Supranox ad.

So when you are trying to persuade someone to protect themselves when they really don't see the need for protection, you can still

succeed if you use the right delivery—the one that creates motivational fit. If they really see little risk from what they are currently
doing—and let's face it, few teenagers do until it's too late—it is better to use promotion-focused messages emphasizing gain to persuade
them than prevention-focused messages emphasizing loss.

## Help Fund Social Initiatives

It's not easy to get people to want to part with their hard-earned money,
particularly in a tough economy. That's true even when the cause is
one we can all agree is a worthy one, like feeding the hungry, shelter-
ing the homeless, or providing a better education for our children. So
when you are an advocate of a worthy cause, you need to do more than
simply plead your case—you need to do it as persuasively as possible.
Once again, the key is understanding the motivational focus of your
target audience and delivering your message in *their* language.

To get a really clear sense of how this works, take a look at the
following essay we created as part of a study (led by our MSC colleague Joe Cesario) advocating the funding of a new after-school
program for students in New York City.[3] Pay close attention to the
subtle shifts in language throughout, and note that the details of the
program itself are always *exactly the same*. Again, it's not about the
content of what you are proposing, so much as it is the way you say
it. (The promotion-worded version contained the phrases that appear
below in italics, while the prevention-worded version substituted the
phrases that appear below in brackets.)

### New Student After-School Program

This essay is written to advocate a new proposed citywide
policy change involving the New York Public School system and

the city of New York. A new city tax would be applied toward the development and implementation of a special after-school program for public grade- and high-school-level students. The primary reason for supporting this program is because it will *advance* [secure] children's education and *support* [prevent] more children *to succeed* [from failing]. If this program is initialized there will be a *greater* [lower] number of schoolchildren who *complete* [fail to complete] the full K–12 education program, and there will be a *greater* [lower] number of students who *succeed* [fail] in their post-academic life choices as well. Given the *higher rate of success* [lower rate of failure] that this program would ensure, it is important to develop this *achievement* [prevention] program as soon as possible.

The primary goal of this program is to *ensure success* [prevent failures] for the city's youth, and it would focus on improving both academic and practical skills. There would be several steps taken to ensure the success of this program in meeting its goal. First, teachers from individual schools would meet to design a program tailored specifically to the needs of that student body. After faculty and administration identified factors which would help *promote achievement* [avert failure] of students at that school, they would design a program which focused specifically on these domain topics. However, the content of a given program would not be limited to any specific topic. Assistance for any issue that the student believes would *help him or her succeed* [prevent him or her from failing] can be addressed in these sessions. Thus, special training could be provided in nearly any academic and relevant practical domain. This design allows for the program to be both specific and broad in terms of the targeted topics that *promote* [prevent] student success.

Another noteworthy aspect of this program will be its comprehensive content, which will include both academic and nonacademic domains. In this way, a broader scope of topics necessary for *success* [the prevention of failure] can be covered. The program, therefore, will focus not only on important academic qualities but also on important social aspects of a student's life. Assistance can be provided for students who wish to receive help with interpersonal skills, emotional difficulties, or any number of social and psychological issues with which they may need help. In addition to the standard academic skills covered in such programs, other less-emphasized topics can be targeted as well; these include topics such as the creative arts (music, painting, etc.), industrial arts (woodworking, mechanics, etc.), home economics, and others. Such a broad skill base allows for the development of the whole person, not just single aspects of one's life. Given this far-reaching knowledge base, student *success* [failure] levels will be *greater* [smaller] because all aspects of the individual can be refined.

Another step taken to ensure the success of this program will be the method by which students are selected to participate. Students can either decide by themselves that they wish to participate in the program or can be recommended for participation by a teacher or administrator. Utilizing both methods of participation will *allow a greater number of students* [prevent less students from missing the opportunity] to participate, and therefore there will be a *higher* [lower] percentage of students *succeeding* [failing] following implementation of the program.

Finally, it is important to consider the issue of the extra tax needed to fund this project. The personal cost of funding this program is far outweighed by the many potential *benefits* [costs] this program will *promote* [avert]. In fact it is estimated that for every dollar spent on this program now, 3.5 extra dollars will be *available in the future due to higher safety rates* [saved in future costs due to lower crime rates] and *greater* [lower] numbers of people *lacking* [with] financial assistance needs. *Greater student successes* [Reduced student failures] now result in *greater benefits* [reduced costs] for everyone, including those same students and other citizens, later.

In conclusion, it is important that we develop and back a special after-school program for the grade- and high-school-level students of NYC, to be funded by a new citywide tax. *By helping students to achieve* [By preventing the failure of students to meet] their academic and social potential, we will have a *greater* [lower] number of students *succeeding* [failing] in both academic and post-academic life. This includes an *increased* [decreased] number of students *finishing* [failing to finish] their K–12 education program, a *greater* [smaller] number of students *attending* [not attending] post–high school education programs, and, overall, *students receiving* [less students failing to receive] more fulfilling and higher-paying jobs. This program can be an effective way of providing the assistance needed to students to *raise* [lower] the overall level of *success* [failure] in our public school system.

Did these subtle differences matter? You bet they did. Dominant promotion or prevention participants who read the version that provided a better fit to their focus (i.e., the promotion or prevention language, respectively) rated the essay as significantly more effective and persuasive and had a much more positive opinion overall of the proposed program, as well as greater willingness to pay to support it. Now that you know how to identify the focus of *your* audience (for a refresher, see chapter 8), you can use this same simple strategy to more effectively advocate for your own worthy cause.

To do so, write out your arguments in whatever way you would normally write them. Next, scan each of your sentences for key promotion- or prevention-focused words or phrases (e.g., *achieve, grow, advance* vs. *prevent, secure, deteriorate*). Ask yourself, is this sentence referring to the potential for gain (e.g., greater success) or for avoiding loss (e.g., less failure)? Rework each sentence, when necessary, so that they all point in the same motivational "direction." The more consistent you are, the more persuasive your appeal is likely to be for the target audience.

Being good at tailoring to fit takes practice . . . like everything else. Even newer members of the MSC who know the research very well sometimes slip in some prevention-focused language when the fit is intended to be with a promotion audience. Indeed, we ourselves still need to double-check our messages for consistency. But you will get better and better at this with practice, and thus more and more effective.

## Stop Tax Cheats

As we've shown, motivational fit comes in very handy when you want to influence other people's intentions—even when that intention is to stop doing something they are very tempted to do, like stop smoking when they are tempted to smoke. Using the right language even works to influence intentions when it comes to doing something you would rather *not* do, like pay your taxes. And there are an awful lot of people out there who aren't paying theirs. In 2006 (the most recent year for which we have data), the IRS reported that 17 percent of income tax owed to the federal government went unpaid. That's about $450 billion of revenue that citizens and businesses in the United States are failing to cough up.

It's easy to sympathize, since few of us really enjoy paying our taxes, and many feel that our current system of taxation is less than fair. Still, governments need taxes in order to provide services, and unpaid taxes mean fewer or inferior services for all of us. So if you were the IRS, how would you try to encourage people to pay their due? A study recently conducted in Austria may provide some valuable guidance (and another great example for this book, since it involved motivational fit).

The Austrian researchers gave a large group of middle-aged taxpayers one of two versions of an appeal, ostensibly from the Austrian Ministry of Finances, to pay their full income taxes (below are translations from the originals). Each began with the following introductory information:

> Citizens' tax payments are the most important source of the state's revenue. In 2005, Austria had total revenues based on taxes, dues and fees of €58.97 billion. Thereof, €31.8 billion were so-called transfer payments. The federation did not use them for fulfilling its own tasks but redistributed them in many ways in the form of public goods and services to the citizens.

Following the introduction, the promotion-focused version continued:

> Paying tax is making the state prosperous. If citizens honestly report to the tax office, the state is able to use the tax budget for financing and improving the welfare system and to provide its citizens with modern health care. Furthermore, if tax payments are sufficient, the state can extend infrastructure such as the road and railway system. The legal system can also be brought to a high and modern level and the safety of the state can be guaranteed. With public money, the educational system can be of high quality and offer a broad learning opportunity at schools and

universities. As for arts and culture, a broad range of events can be subsidized. All citizens profit from public goods and services if taxpayers pay tax honestly.

In contrast, following the same introduction, the prevention-focused version continued:

Without paying tax no state can prosper. If citizens do not report to the tax office honestly, tax revenue is low and the state is no longer able to care about social justice and equal medical treatment for all citizens. Furthermore, if tax payments are insufficient, the state has to cut down on infrastructure; the continuous maintenance of the road and railway system can no longer be guaranteed. Extensive economies could impend in the field of security and the legal system. If public money is not enough, the educational system could deteriorate and the standard of schools and universities could decrease. As for arts and culture, a shortage of subsidies strongly curtails the cultural offer. Citizens profit less from public goods and services if a major part of the taxpayers evade.

Next, everyone was asked to imagine that they had received a gift of 4,500 euros, and that they planned to use the money to buy a new car. If they chose to report the gift income to the government, they would owe taxes on it and therefore have less left to buy the car. If they didn't report the money and were caught, they would have to pay a fine—but it was pointed out that the chances of being caught were quite low (which, generally speaking, is true).

When promotion-minded Austrians read about the *benefits* for everyone when the number of people who pay their taxes is high, they had stronger intentions to pay the tax they owed, while prevention-minded Austrians were much more motivated to pay the tax when they learned about how everyone would *suffer* when the number of taxpayers is low.[4]

Sometimes people just need a little bit of a nudge to do the right thing—the kind that motivational fit can easily provide. Anyone who is teetering on the fence about going to the polls to vote, separating their recycling, getting a flu shot, conserving water, or any of the countless other things they know they are better off doing but don't really want to do, may finally *feel* like it's the right thing to do if they experience fit when considering doing it.

## Why We Need a Good Fit Now More Than Ever

There are so many messages vying for our attention at almost every moment of our waking lives. We carry on conversations with one another while also glancing frequently at our smartphones, while the TV blares in the background. We read a magazine while also listening to our MP3 players, while glancing up occasionally at the other people and the ads in the subway car. We drive while listening to talk radio, reading the billboards as they zoom by. All this information is trying hard to worm its way into our brains—but what actually makes it in? To say "not much" would be an understatement. Barely any of it gets in and really sticks.

Because of this, there's no time like the present for mastering the art and science of creating motivational fit. At the conclusion of the most recent edition of *Influence*, Cialdini remarks on the evolution of technology and the overload of information we each have to slog through daily—all those e-mails, commercials, Facebook posts, and Tweets—and how these changes affect the art of persuasion. "When making a decision," he writes, "we will less frequently enjoy the luxury of a fully considered analysis of the total situation but will revert increasingly to a focus on a single, usually reliable feature of it." As we hope we have illustrated through the examples in *Focus*, motivational fit creates just such a reliable feature to guide our decisions—the experience of *feeling right*.

If you would like the information you are conveying to elbow its way past all that competition, you need every advantage. Which is why people spend a fortune on eye-catching ads, celebrity endorsements, and premium ad space. But all the money in the world, all by itself, won't make your message *feel right* to your audience. When something feels right, it grabs your attention and will be remembered. To make sure your time, effort, and money are well spent, make sure you're delivering a message with fit.

# CHAPTER 12

## To Market

A THIRTY-SECOND COMMERCIAL SPOT DURING THE 2012 SUPER Bowl cost an average of $3.5 million, not including the cost of actually making the commercial. Advertising—whether on television, by radio, in print, or on the Web—is expensive. The vast majority of the billions upon billions of dollars spent by U.S. companies each year on ads is spent with a single purpose in mind: to get you to *buy* something. There are an awful lot of people out there whose job it is to persuade you to choose their product over some alternative, and the stakes for them are very high. The advertiser who delivers its pitch with motivational fit will have an advantage in this crowded field. In this chapter, we'll show you why.

### Fit Makes You *Really* Want It

Everything starts with intentions. The road to Hell may be paved with them, but we must not forget that the road to Heaven is paved with them, too. Without the intention to do something (consciously *or* unconsciously), nothing happens. Which is why changing (or creating) intentions is the first—and very necessary—step in the process of influencing others to buy your product. They've got to *want* it—whatever "it" may be. This, ultimately, is why things like brand attitude and perceptions of value matter—they affect our *intention* to buy Coke rather than Pepsi, or to see the new Russell Crowe action flick over the new Ben Stiller romantic comedy.

Experiencing motivational fit when we read, watch, or listen to an advertisement has a direct and measurable effect on our intentions. One of us (Grant Halvorson) has frequently noticed the influence of fit when it comes to her own purchases. She explains:

As I've mentioned already, in my personal life I am pretty consistently prevention-focused. I want whatever is safe, reliable, and not too expensive. I distrust advertising. I read the negative reviews first when I am shopping online, to see how bad the product's faults are and whether or not I can live with them. And I couldn't care less about being cool, if cool costs a fortune and won't stand the test of time. So I am generally turned off by ads that try to make practical, functional purchases sound hip or luxurious—like minivans (the Toyota Sienna is a *swagger wagon?*) or toilet paper (Charmin wants me to *Enjoy the Go?*).

There is one important exception, however: *technology.* I am a promotion-focused technology dork—the kind of person who gets excited about each and every new advance in e-readers, tablets, laptops, smartphones, and wireless accessibility. I own a Kindle *and* a Nook, an iPad, several iPods, four laptops, and more smartphones than I am comfortable discussing publicly. I have spent an embarrassing amount of money over the years on all the latest gizmos, only to find that many of them either did not really deliver on their promises or stopped working correctly with alarming speed. None of these bad experiences have remotely dampened my passion for the newest iWhatever, much to my husband's chagrin. All the advertising strategies that normally don't work on me when I'm shopping for *anything* else seem utterly compelling when I've got my eye on a gadget. (Hmm, the new iPad has a "stunning" display with "richer" details, and an "ultrafast" 4G wireless connection? *That feels right.*)

When we experience motivational fit from an advertisement, it increases our engagement with—and *commitment* to—choosing that product. Drinking Welch's grape juice "to get energized" fits with promotion motivation, because it's an *eager* strategy—so you feel right about it. ("Come on, let's get energized!" just sounds exciting, doesn't it? When you are promotion-focused, that's what you want—excitement, luxury, and innovation.) You like the brand more, so you have a stronger intention to buy it the next time you are wandering the aisles of your supermarket.

On the other hand, drinking Welch's grape juice "to avoid missing out on getting energized" does *not* fit your promotion motivation, because it's a *vigilant* strategy. It's about not making a mistake—which, to the promotion-focused, is a nonfit message that feels wrong. "Don't miss out on getting energized!" sounds a little weird if you're promotion-minded. If that is Welch's message, it will diminish your intention to drink it and you will like the brand less. Suddenly, Ocean Spray will look like a better choice.

But what if you are prevention-minded? In that case, you are a lot more sensitive to screwing up. You really don't want to make a mistake, so "Don't miss out on getting energized!" doesn't sound weird to you at all. In fact, it sounds convincing. Hearing that it would be a mistake *not* to drink it will strengthen your intention to buy Welch's grape juice, and you will like the brand more. Welch's will now feel like the *right* choice.[1]

## Five Out of Five Consumers Prefer Fit

Imagine that you are on your way to a week-long Caribbean vacation, so you head to the local pharmacy to pick up a few things for the trip, including some sunscreen. When you get to the sunscreen display, you see that there are two major brands to choose from: Brand X and Brand Y.

Brand X's label says:
*Give sunburn no chance. Brand X provides safe protection. Brand X—the double protection.*
Brand Y's label says:
*Enjoy the warm rays of the sun. Brand Y for a healthy tan. Brand Y—enjoy the sun.*

Which is more appealing? Which one would *you* buy? Which one do you think our nervous friend Jon (who, incidentally, isn't all that outdoorsy) would buy? The researchers found that overall, people tend to prefer Brand X—not surprising, since the act of using sunscreen is inherently more prevention-focused than promotion-focused. Its primary function, after all, is to *protect* your skin by screening out the sun. But that's not all the researchers found; among buyers like Jon who also have a dominant prevention motivation, the preference for Brand X was significantly stronger than among buyers with a dominant promotion motivation.[2] So here we see again two separate sources of motivational fit working simultaneously:

1. The prevention-focused description of Brand X fits with the prevention-focused purpose that sunscreen, as a product, serves (i.e., skin protection)

and

2. The prevention-focused description of Brand X fits with the dominant motivation of the prevention-focused buyers

Matching the framing of the ad to the motivation of the audience, or to the motivation the product was designed to serve, has also been shown to improve brand attitudes toward supplements,[3] elliptical trainers,[4] toothpaste,[5] and, as we mentioned earlier, grape juice.[6] Whenever we make one brand feel *right* compared to another, we're making it more likely to be the one people will choose.

You can also create a *third* source of fit if you talk about the means of reaching the goal (i.e., protecting the skin) in a way that also fits with prevention motivation. When a fictional sunscreen brand, Sunskin, was described in prevention-focused terms . . .

*Be safe! Know that you are risk free from sunburns, feeling completely relaxed.*

Consumers had even more positive brand attitudes when the tagline was *also* loss-framed,

*Don't miss out on being safe.*

rather than gain-framed,

*Be safe.*

"Don't miss out on being safe" fits with prevention because it is a *vigilant* strategy—stay on the alert, use this product, and you won't make a mistake.

Fit can also be an effective way to position your product to an undertapped segment of the market—people who, up until now, just haven't been interested in what you are selling. To illustrate what we mean, let's take the example of health insurance.

## Appealing to New Audiences Through Fit

At first glance, a product like health insurance (really, *any* kind of insurance) would appear to be a quintessentially prevention-focused product, designed to help you avoid financial problems following some misfortune or disaster. But insurance is really a risk-*sharing* product—you take on some of the risk, the insurer takes on the rest—and customers can choose plans with levels of coverage that provide relatively more or less risk protection.

To avoid larger risks, customers can choose "Cadillac" plans that have high premiums but low deductibles (the amount that the insured person must pay out of pocket before the insurer pays for anything) and low copays (an amount paid by the insured person for each medical service). You pay a larger fee each month, but at least you know with certainty that this is *all* you will pay if some misfortune does happen. This kind of plan is a prevention-focused product, since its benefits lie primarily in avoiding any ugly surprises. It will appeal most to prevention-minded consumers and should be advertised most effectively with *loss* framing, like:

*If you don't choose this plan, you may have to shell out a lot of money if you become seriously ill.*

Lower-monthly-premium, higher-risk plans leave more money in consumers' budgets for things that are a lot more fun than insurance, but if they are sick they are responsible for more of the costs they may incur—higher copays and deductibles. This kind of plan is more promotion-focused, because it involves accepting risk in exchange for the reward of cheaper premiums that frees up money for alternative pursuits. Basically, it's a gamble. And as such, it will appeal most to promotion-minded consumers and be most effectively marketed using *gain* framing:

*If you choose this plan, then you will enjoy more money in your pocket each month.*

In fact, a recent study involving customers of a large Dutch insurance company looked at how perceptions of plan value and purchase intentions were influenced by gain versus loss framing, and found that low-premium, high-deductible (promotion) plans were indeed more appealing when gain framed, while high-premium, no-deductible (prevention) plans benefited more from loss framing.[7]

(Note: A product's "cheapness" could also be framed in a way that appeals to the prevention-minded—e.g., "avoid a large monthly payment"—but when the product in question achieves lower costs *by increasing potential risk*, it makes for an unappealing combination to a consumer looking to remain safe not just now but well into the future.)

Increasing motivational fit may become especially valuable to insurers trying to capture a new segment of the market: all the individuals who will be forced for the first time to purchase insurance as a result of health care reform (whether at the national level or the state level). Very roughly, half of those who don't have insurance (many millions) are without it by choice—technically, they could afford the premiums or are eligible for Medicaid, but choose instead to take the risk of paying out of pocket. This willingness to accept risk suggests that, motivationally speaking, these people are promotion-minded with respect to their finances. Many are what health insurers refer to as the "Young Invincibles"—young males who aren't terribly worried about the odds of getting saddled with a big hospital bill. Since Young Invincibles do, in fact, tend to have relatively low annual medical costs, they are a particularly desirable population to add to any health insurer's roster. To capture this new promotion-focused market, it's not enough to plaster your website with "cool" images of snowboarders and popular athletes if you are just going to offer them the same prevention-focused products that you offer to your older consumers. The options available to Young Invincibles should always be *gain* framed—emphasizing benefits, bonuses, and rewards.

## Appealing to Different Cultures Through Fit

The culturally based differences in promotion and prevention focus we described back in chapter 8 also have significant implications for how products are marketed, or should be marketed, to different societies (and to different segments of the same society). Advertisements that provide "fit" for people raised in one place, or who view the "self" in one way, may not work so well in a different setting. For instance, one study found that people with a more American-like, independent self-view preferred (fictional) SunUp orange juice more when it was advertised using promotion-focused language:

*Building strong hearts, one glass at a time. SunUp is the orange juice you can count on to promote your healthy heart.*

Those with a more Asian-like, interdependent self-view preferred SunUp orange juice more when it was described in prevention-focused terms:

*Preventing weak hearts, one glass at a time. SunUp is the orange juice you can count on to protect your heart.*

Another study showed that gain framing an appeal to floss regularly (i.e., emphasizing the rewards of flossing) was more effective for white British consumers, while loss framing (i.e., emphasizing the costs of *not* flossing) worked better for East Asian consumers.[8] U.S. advertisers, who must typically market to a wide variety of ethnic and cultural groups across the country, would be wise to target ads using the right motivational language to different communities.

## Fit Loosens the Purse Strings

Sure, experiencing motivational fit leads people to have stronger intentions and like your ideas or products more—but let's talk dollars. Will fit make a product seem like it's worth *paying more* for? Absolutely. To prove it, let's take a look at one of the earliest motivational fit studies run at the Motivation Science Center ten years ago, in which we asked Columbia undergrads, ostensibly as part of a marketing study on consumer preferences, to choose between a mug and a pen.[9] The choice itself was a bit rigged—the mug was much nicer than the pen and was preferred by almost everyone. We wanted there to be a strong preference for the mug, so that we could see how fit influenced the monetary value of the *same* preferred choice.

We asked the students to make the decision in one of two ways: by focusing on what they would gain by choosing the mug or the pen (a decision strategy that fits with promotion), or by focusing on what they would lose by *not* choosing the mug or the pen (a decision strategy that fits with prevention). Note that in both cases the students consider the positive qualities of the mug and the pen, but they do so in an *eager* way (e.g., the positive qualities of the mug they would *gain* by choosing it) or in a *vigilant* way (e.g., the positive qualities of the mug they would *not lose* by choosing it). We also measured whether each student was promotion- or prevention-minded in general. After each student chose the mug, we asked, "What do you think is the price of the mug?" As shown below, the perceived price of the mug was much greater—*50 percent greater*—when the decision was made with fit rather than with nonfit.

|  | Choice based on gains | Choice based on avoiding losses |
|---|---|---|
| Promotion-focused choosers | $8.78 | $6.32 |
| Prevention-focused choosers | $5.00 | $8.07 |

Note: Shaded boxes are the choices made with motivational fit.

You might be saying to yourself, "But the measure of value in this study was the *perceived price* of the mug. What if they actually had to spend their own money to buy it? Would fit have such a big effect . . . or any effect at all?" Fair question, and one that occurred to us as well. With another group of students, we gave each of them five dollars at the beginning of the study and then we repeated the same procedure. Once again the students chose the mug over the pen. We then showed them an envelope that contained a fair price for the mug, and told them that they could buy the mug if they wished to, but only if they offered an amount that was equal to or higher than the price in the envelope (the idea is similar to a silent auction—you make your best bid and see what happens). If they offered an amount less than the price, they would not get the mug. If they offered an amount equal to or higher than the price in the envelope, they would get the mug *for the price that they offered*. The table below shows how much of *their own five dollars* they were willing to pay to get the mug in each condition.

| | Choice based on gains | Choice based on avoiding losses |
|---|---|---|
| Promotion-minded choosers | $4.76 | $3.11 |
| Prevention-minded choosers | $2.49 | $4.68 |

Note: Shaded boxes are the choices made with motivational fit.

So the answer is "Yes!" Even when people are spending their own money to buy their chosen object they will offer much more when they make their decision in a way that creates motivational fit. Indeed, the effect of fit is, if anything, even greater when they are deciding how much to spend of their *own* money to buy it (in the second study). Fit is an experience that creates real, honest-to-goodness cash value. Findings like these have been replicated with many other kinds of products, too. For instance, when consumers were allowed to evaluate bike helmets in a way that created motivational fit, they were willing to pay about 20 percent more for one than when they experienced nonfit.[10] In yet another study, consumers offered to pay more than 40 percent more for the same reading book light if the way they made their choice created fit versus nonfit.[11]

At this point, you might be wondering whether fit is creating an illusion that affects choices and perceived value separate from actual experienced value. If so, wouldn't it be wrong to give people such an imaginary inflated sense of a product's value? We agree that it would be wrong. But that's *not* what motivational fit does, because the increase in value is *real*. In other words, people not only pay more for the mug—they experience it as a genuinely better mug. That's because motivational fit also affects how satisfied people are with the choices they've made. So our promotion-focused friend Ray will be happier with the car he buys when he makes his decision eagerly ("This car has great mileage!"), while prevention-focused Jon will feel best when he makes his decision vigilantly ("I can't afford to pass up this car's great mileage!").

Unlike so many of the more manipulative techniques employed by unscrupulous salespeople, motivational fit isn't a dirty trick to be played on an unsuspecting consumer. Whether you are talking about mugs, computers, or electric grills, study after study shows that consumers who choose products while *feeling right* are later significantly more satisfied with their selections.[12] So if you are in the advertising business, where the products can be political candidates as well as toothpaste, and you use motivational fit to make your ads more persuasive, it is important to remember that fit increases the *experienced value* of things—not just what things are chosen or how much people are willing to pay for them.

## CHAPTER 13

# A Step-by-Step Guide to Creating Motivational Fit

THERE ARE THREE SIMPLE STEPS TO CREATING FIT. TO GIVE YOU A better sense of how the process works, imagine for a moment that you are on the school board in a community where school budgets are subject to a public vote. *You need to convince your neighbors that an increase in property taxes is justified for necessary improvements in the schools.* Now it's time to choose the right language.

## Step 1: Find Their Focus

You start by asking, *What does my audience want?* What is their motivation with respect to this issue? What is *their* goal? In this instance, you are targeting an entire community. You have more than one audience, so you need to identify the dominant motivational focus of each major group.

Parents of school-aged children, for instance, will have a lot to gain from better-funded schools. After all, they want their kids to have every opportunity for growth and advancement. So with respect to the issue of increasing school budgets (from a property tax increase), they are likely to be more promotion-focused.

Retirees, on the other hand, are by necessity focused on their own financial security. Many are on a fixed income and want to protect what they already have. As a result, they are likely to approach the issue of a property tax increase (to increase school budgets) with more of a prevention focus. (Also, as we told you in chapter 8, older people are more prevention-minded on average than younger people.) These two very different motivational focuses will require two different messages using different language to create a good fit with each audience.

## Step 2: Craft Content That Fits

Next, figure out exactly what you want your audience to *do*, and whether that action or decision is naturally more *promotion-focused or prevention-focused, or if it could it be either*. (Most of the time, it could be either. In other words, most of what we do in the course of our everyday lives could be motivated by either promotion or prevention concerns. But every once in a while there's something like "getting a flu shot," which is awfully hard to describe in a promotion-focused way.)

You know what you want your audience to do—you want them all to vote yes on a property tax increase to increase the school budgets. Regarding the motivational focus that underlies this decision, in this case it can be either promotion or prevention motivated—you could argue that a property tax increase for improving the schools will bring about advancement and opportunity *or* help to enhance community safety and security.

So for the promotion-focused parents of school-aged kids, you'll want a promotion-focused message that describes how paying more to support schools will provide the *best*, most *ideal* learning environment for their children. This, incidentally, is the kind of argument school boards usually make, which is why parents nearly always vote yes on school budgets.

The retirees with their prevention focus are a bit trickier (which is why they notoriously vote no on school budgets). The key to crafting message content for them is to think about how paying more for schools could help them reach their goal of being more *secure*, to make them believe that voting no would be a *mistake*. For example, a message that emphasizes how communities with better schools have less crime and stable property values would be prevention-focused. So, too, would pointing out that necessary improvements will only get *more* expensive if they are not addressed immediately—so paying a bit more now is a way to avoid a bigger *loss* down the road (e.g., "It would be a big mistake to wait until things really get bad").

(As we discussed earlier in the book, when you don't know the focus of your audience, your best bet is to craft a message that contains elements that will appeal to each focus—some arguments that fit promotion and some that fit prevention. This will usually be somewhat less effective than a perfectly targeted message, but it will be more effective than a single-focus message that misses half your audience or some general non-focus-tailored message.)

## Step 3: Deliver Your Message with Language That Fits

Now that you've got your two messages for your two audiences, it's time to decide how you'll deliver those messages in a way that creates even more motivational fit. You've got *ten* delivery methods that will do the trick.

## Delivery Method #1: Frame It in Terms of Gain or Loss

This one you know by heart, right? Gain framing emphasizes advancements (moving to "+1") from taking the action or buying the product (e.g., how your toothpaste provides a *gain* like a whiter smile or becoming cavity free). Loss framing emphasizes how things could get worse (moving to "−1") from *not* taking the action or buying the product (e.g., without your toothpaste, you'll experience a *loss* like your smile being less white or an increase in cavities). Let's apply this delivery method to our school budget example:

### Version 1: Promotion + Gain Framing

Vote YES on the School Budget!

Vote YES and we can create the best possible learning environment and provide the most opportunities for our community's children.

> *Analysis:* This version creates the most fit for parents of school-aged kids. Use this one.

### Version 2: Promotion + Loss Framing

Don't Vote NO on the School Budget!

Vote NO, and we will lose the chance to maintain a good learning environment or provide the needed opportunities for our community's children.

> *Analysis:* This creates a nonfit experience for the parents of school-aged kids. Don't use this one.

### Version 3: Prevention + Gain Framing

Vote YES on the School Budget!
Vote YES and we can make our school and community safer. We can make progress against crime and maintain property values.

*Analysis:* This version creates a nonfit experience for the retirees. Don't use this one.

### Version 4: Prevention + Loss Faming

Don't Vote NO on the School Budget!
Vote NO, and we won't be able to maintain a safe school and community. We won't be able to keep crime low and property values stable.

*Analysis:* This version creates the most fit for the retirees. Use this one.

Here are some more examples you can refer to when you want to use Delivery Method #1, to help you get the language just right.

|  | Approach Gain | Avoid Loss |
|---|---|---|
| **Selling Mugs** | Think about what you gain if you choose this mug. | Think about what you lose if you don't choose this mug. |
| **Soccer Practice** | Your aspiration is to score at least three times out of five. | Your obligation is to miss no more than two times out of five. |
| **Get Healthy!** | These are the benefits of being active . . . | These are the costs of being inactive . . . |
| **School Budget** | Why you should vote yes. | Why you shouldn't vote no. |
| **Classroom Feedback** | The benefits of studying. | Costs of not studying. |
| **Workplace Incentives** | Good things that happen when you meet sales targets. | Bad things that happen when you don't meet sales targets. |

## Delivery Method #2: Emphasize Why or How

As we mentioned back in chapter 6, promotion-focused people tend to think in more abstract terms, while prevention-focused people prefer concrete ways of thinking. Because promotion is about hopes and dreams for the future, it makes people see the big picture and perceive things globally. In contrast, because prevention is about being careful to maintain the current satisfactory state, it makes people pay attention to the details of what is happening now, perceiving things more locally and looking out for possible problems.[1]

One way to make your message either abstract or concrete is to focus on why versus how. If you are promotion-focused, you want to know *why* you should do something (e.g., why should I invest in this mutual fund?), but if you are prevention-focused, it's more about *how* (e.g., how exactly does this mutual fund work?). So when you deliver your message in *why* language, it creates fit for promotion. Delivering it in *how* language will create fit for prevention. Below, you can find more examples to guide you when using this technique.

| | Why | How |
|---|---|---|
| **Selling Mugs** | With this Columbia mug, you can show your school pride! | This generous, fifteen-ounce mug is made from a shatter-proof material. |
| **Soccer Practice** | Let's become the best team in the league! | Let's stay focused on the techniques needed to penetrate their strong defenses. |
| **Get Healthy!** | Regular exercise will leave you looking and feeling great! | Regular exercise burns calories and raises your metabolism. |
| **School Budget** | The proposed tax increase will give our children new opportunities to learn and develop! | The proposed tax increase will fund a new after-school tutoring program and the hiring of five new teachers. |

*(continued)*

|  | Why | How |
|---|---|---|
| **Classroom Feedback** | If you work hard in class, you'll open doors to new opportunities in the future. | If you work hard in class, you'll get the grades you need to avoid rejection by top colleges. |
| **Workplace Incentives** | The best performers will quickly rise to the top! | The top three performers will maintain their chance for a promotion this year. |

## Delivery Method #3: Use Adjectives or Verbs

Another way to manipulate the abstractness of your message is to make *the words themselves* more abstract. Work in psycholinguistics has demonstrated that adjectives are the most abstract language category, because they generalize across specific events (e.g., "A is aggressive"), whereas action verbs are the most concrete language category because they contextualize and situate the event (e.g., "A punches B").[2] In a study by Gun Semin and his colleagues, this technique was used to increase the effectiveness of messages advocating playing sports. The benefits of playing sports were described either by using abstract adjectives (e.g., "Doing sports is good for you. . . . Sports make your muscles and bones *stronger*, and gives you a *better* functioning heart and lungs") or by using concrete action verbs (e.g., "Doing sports is good for you. . . . Exercising *strengthens* your muscles and bones, and *improves* how your heart and lungs function").

The researchers found that the participants were significantly more motivated to engage in sports after reading the message when the language fit their dominant focus (abstract for dominant promotion; concrete for dominant prevention). Very subtle changes in parts of speech were enough to create fit and increase motivation—which means that all those elementary school grammar lessons can finally come in handy.[3]

## Delivery Method #4: Highlight Succeeding or Not Failing

Thinking about how well things went in the past, or how well they are going to go in the future, does wonders for the self-confidence of the promotion-minded. Promotion motivation thrives on a confident, sunny outlook. For people with a dominant promotion focus, positive feedback yields superior performance,[4] and optimism is a strong predictor of well-being and life satisfaction.[5] So delivering your message in upbeat, gray-skies-are-gonna-clear-up language and tone is another great way to create fit. And as we mentioned earlier, promotion-focused people are also more motivated by *inspirational role models*. Stories or images of other people's successes can be as motivating as their own past successes.

Prevention motivation, on the other hand, is enhanced when we think about times in our past when we failed from not being prepared enough, or when we worry about what might happen in the future—when things could go wrong if we are not careful enough or don't work hard enough. For people with a dominant prevention focus, what yields the best performance is *negative* feedback that maintains vigilance . . . not mean or even critical feedback, but feedback that you could fail if you don't try hard enough.[6] So delivering your message with more prudent, it-could-rain language and tone is the way to create fit for them. They are also more motivated by *cautionary tales*—sometimes, you really can learn from (and be motivated by) other people's mistakes. Importantly, these messages are not pessimistic . . . they are not saying that something bad *will* happen to you. Instead, they are saying that something bad *might* happen to you if you are not careful to do what's necessary to stop it from happening.

## Delivery Method #5: Emphasize Change or Stability

By emphasizing how a product or action represents either change or stability, you have yet another way to effectively create fit for your audience. A detergent that contains "a breakthrough advance in biochemistry for removing stains in a whole new way" will sound right to a promotion-focused shopper, while a detergent that "has been a trusted stain fighter that moms have turned to for generations" will sound right to someone more prevention-focused. (Promotion-focused people also tend to think the future is more important than the present, so messages that are forward-looking will be particularly persuasive to them.)[7]

## Delivery Method #6: Describe It as Taking a Chance or Being Cautious

Somewhere between being a professional daredevil (hyperpromotion) and hiding in your own underground panic room (hyperprevention) is where most of us live our lives. Much of what we do each day involves a mixture of taking chances and being cautious and can be described using either side of the coin. If you think your promotion-focused teenager should apply to at least ten colleges to be on the "safe" side (a conservative, prevention-focused approach that *you* prefer), you should probably describe it to him in riskier terms to fit his promotion motivation. ("Hey, why not *take a chance* and go for lots of schools? It's a gamble, but it could pay off and leave you with lots of options!") On the other hand, if your teenager is prevention-focused and wants to play it "safe," then cautious language is what you want to make applying to ten or more schools feel right. ("To reduce the chance of ending up in a college you don't like, or in no college at all, you need to apply to at least ten schools, including several 'safety' schools.")

## Delivery Method #7: Emphasize Feelings or Reasons

Messages that ask people to consult their feelings when making a decision provide a good fit for promotion. Prevention-focused people, on the other hand, prefer to make their decisions based on logic and reason. In fact, one study found that promotion- and prevention-focused consumers were willing to pay on average 45 *percent more* for the product they chose when they were told, respectively, to choose it based on how they felt emotionally when exposed to each product (emphasizing feelings) or to choose it based on evaluative ratings of each product for different qualities (emphasizing reasons).[8]

### Promotion-Focused Appeals to Feelings

*Think about how it makes you feel.*
*Go with your instinct.*
*You'll just know it's right for you.*

### Prevention-Focused Appeals to Reasons

*Studies show that . . .*
*Make the smart choice . . .*
*The evidence is in. . . .*

## Delivery Method # 8: Use Animated or Reserved Gestures

It's not just what you say verbally that can create fit (or nonfit), it's also *how* you say it *nonverbally*. As our Motivation Science Center colleague Joe Cesario discovered, the way you move your hands, how you position your body, and the speed with which you speak can all affect the motivational fit of your message and how persuasive it will be to your audience.[9]

*Eager gesturing* is animated. It involves using broad, open hand movements with fingers spread wide, projecting outward—away from your body. Your body leans forward, toward the listener, and you speak and move your hands quickly. This kind of body language fits with promotion motivation—it's bold, fast, and forward-moving.

*Vigilant gesturing* is more reserved. It involves precise, closed hand movements with fingers close together and motions that appear to be "pushing" back toward the listener (as if to say "slow down!"). Your body leans backward, away from the listener, and you speak and move your hands slowly. This kind of body language fits with prevention motivation—it's careful, precise, and deliberate.

## Delivery Method # 9: Emphasize the Parts or the Whole

Back in chapter 6, we told you that promotion-focused people generally prefer to compare products or options through *holistic processing*—considering each product or option as a whole before moving on to the next one. Prevention-focused people instead prefer *attribute processing*—considering every product along a single dimension, and then moving on to the next dimension. By presenting choices in different ways, influencers can use this knowledge to design messages that create motivational fit.

Consider two laptops, Alpha and Beta. Imagine you are the maker of the Alpha laptop and you want to show potential customers how it stands up against its rival, the Beta. If you have reason to believe your customers are more promotion-focused (say, because they are younger, or because your brand is seen as cutting-edge and innovative), you could choose to present the information in a *holistic processing* format where you show everything about each laptop separately, like this one:

### Alpha Laptop

1.6 GHz dual-core Intel processor
3 GB memory
weighs only 3 pounds
13" screen
available in custom colors
    price: $999.99

### Beta Laptop

2.0 GHz dual-core Intel processor
5 GB memory
weighs only 5.6 pounds
13" screen
available in black or silver
    price: $1,299.99

But if your audience is more prevention-focused (if, for example, they are a bit older, or your brand is known for its reliability and helpful customer service), they would experience fit from receiving it in an *attribute processing* format where you directly compare the laptops, attribute by attribute, as follows:

|           | ALPHA Laptop            | BETA Laptop             |
|-----------|-------------------------|-------------------------|
| Processor | 1.6 GHz dual core Intel | 2.0 GHz dual core Intel |
| Memory    | 3 GB                    | 5 GB                    |
| Weight    | 3 pounds                | 5.6 pounds              |
| Screen    | 13"                     | 13"                     |
| Colors    | custom                  | black or silver         |
| Price     | $999.99                 | $1299.99                |

Once again, these simple choices in message delivery really matter. Prevention-minded people who were able to consider products in attribute-processing format and promotion-minded people who were given the more holistic option were significantly more satisfied with their choices and were willing to pay roughly 20 percent more for them.[10]

## Delivery Method #10: Let Fit Rub Off

When all else fails and you can't quite figure out how to create motivational fit for your product or idea, you can actually still experience its benefits through something we call *transfer of fit*. Studies show that the feeling of "rightness" and strengthened engagement created by a motivational fit sticks around for a while. And people are not aware of where their motivational experiences are coming from. So if people experience fit immediately *before* hearing about your message, the message could benefit from fit's "rightness" or strengthened engagement.

Take, for example, a study conducted by Higgins and MSC Fellows Lorraine Chen Idson, Tony Freitas, Scott Spiegel, and Dan Molden.[11] In one study, the participants were given a packet of questionnaires. In an early questionnaire in the packet, the participants made a list of either their hopes or aspirations (creating a promotion focus) or their duties and obligations (creating a prevention focus). Next, they were asked to list strategies to *make sure everything goes right* (a fit for promotion) or to *make sure nothing goes wrong* (a fit for prevention). Later on in the packet they responded to a questionnaire that asked them to look at pictures of three dogs and rate the dogs' "good-naturedness."

Those participants who had listed strategies that fit with their focus (i.e., promotion + make sure everything goes right; prevention + make sure nothing goes wrong) rated the dogs as significantly more good-natured than those who experienced nonfit. So feeling right from motivational fit transferred to feeling right *about the dog*—suddenly Rex seemed like a pretty nice little guy, the kind you would like to play fetch with.

Transfer-of-fit effects have also been demonstrated for both physical and mental performance.[12] Fit can also transfer to feelings of trust. (Not surprisingly, such transfer increases trust in another person more when you don't know the person well and have little actual evidence to go on.)[13] Fit transfer even helps you make better, healthier snacking choices! In one study, participants were given, as a parting gift, a choice between an apple or a chocolate bar. Those who had experienced fit on the previous task chose the apple over the chocolate bar 83 percent of the time, compared to only 20 percent of those who experienced nonfit (and 53 percent of those in a control group).[14] When you feel right from fit, it's easier to summon the willpower to take the healthier option. But when you feel wrong from nonfit, it's even more tempting to seek solace in chocolate.

It is possible, then, to create fit effects on engagement and persuasion not only from what you are doing *now* but also from what you did just moments ago. Thanks to Delivery Method #10, motivational fit as a mechanism for influence has a much broader range of applicability across multiple issues and multiple audiences. You just have to get *near* fit to make the magic happen.

With only three steps, the process of creating motivational fit isn't a particularly elaborate one. Once you've had some practice with it, expressing yourself and your ideas while harnessing fit's power to influence will become second nature. And with ten different delivery methods (which can be used separately, or together to pack a bigger punch), it won't be hard to find the language that works best with your circumstances. You've got the tools at your fingertips to be more influential than ever before, because now you understand the art— and science—of making fit work for you. Remember our simple motto: *It's the fit that counts.*

# Epilogue

PSYCHOLOGY IS A RELATIVELY YOUNG SCIENCE, AS FAR AS SCIENCES go. It was more or less a branch of philosophy until the creation of the first experimental psychology lab in 1879 (by Wilhelm Wundt in Leipzig, followed soon after by laboratories at Johns Hopkins University and the University of Pennsylvania). So it can be forgiven for getting things wrong from time to time. After all, every science evolves. Moreover, there's nothing quite so complicated as the human mind or human behavior, and we haven't been at this for very long.

This book, and the research behind it, is part of an effort to address a mistake psychologists (and people who use psychology to do their jobs—like parents, teachers, managers, and marketers) have been making for a very long time: paying attention to only *half* the story.

Interestingly, it's not always the same half. For example, economists embraced psychological theories like *loss aversion*—which says that people react more strongly to a loss than a gain of equal size, or why it hurts more to have twenty dollars fall out of your wallet than it feels good to find twenty dollars on the street—without realizing that loss aversion is a prevention-focused phenomenon. When people are promotion-focused, they are actually more sensitive to *gains* than losses. So economists in this case are only seeing the prevention half of the story.

The self-help industry, on the other hand, tends to tell only the promotion side of the story. Adherents focus almost entirely on the importance of "happiness" and advocate optimism and positive thinking as the cure for whatever ails you—not realizing that there is more to life than happiness (e.g., peacefulness) and that optimism does *not* work for everyone.

Similarly, advice on how to motivate our young people, our employees, and ourselves is almost always about using *rewards*, like bonuses, to get things going. Which is a great idea, assuming you want to advance or make additional gains rather than maintain security or ensure safety. When people need to be vigilant, or to maintain the satisfactory state they've already established, "carrots" (whatever form they take) are a poor way to keep them motivated. Once again, rewards fit only the promotion half of the story.

Even when an area of study begins with both promotion and prevention being emphasized, it can evolve in a way that ends up with only one motivational focus receiving attention. This was true, for example, of John Bowlby's pioneering work on attachment in children. Bowlby originally emphasized both security (prevention) and nurturance (promotion) as separate survival needs that infants depend on their caretakers to fulfill. Over time, however, the attachment concepts that received the most attention were "safe haven," "secure base," and "fear of strangers," and the attachment styles that children developed were called "secure," "anxious-avoidant," and "anxious-ambivalent." Now the story of parent-child attachment has become mostly a prevention focus story.

Now that you have read *Focus*, you know the whole story. You know that there are two different and distinct sets of lenses we use to see the world, and you know which one you use most. One of the most gratifying aspects of telling people about promotion and prevention is having them tell us how, suddenly, so much *makes sense* that never made sense before. They understand why they are so good at some things and have such a hard time with others. Why there has been so much miscommunication in their workplace, in their marriage, or with their children. Why they can be with another person in the same place at the same time, seeing the very same things, yet experience them so very differently.

Your life is more empowered once you have learned about promotion and prevention focus and what fits with them. This is true, in part, because you realize how you can be much more effective in just about everything you do—by working with what fits your focus, capitalizing on your strengths, and compensating when you can for your weaknesses. Your life is also less frustrating because understanding focus allows you to go a little easier on yourself, and on everyone else. You don't have to be good at everything at every moment, because you realize you can't be. *No one can.* Promotion and prevention will always have trade-offs. And you are less surprised by, and less bothered by, the people who use a different set of lenses than you usually do; they are much less annoying because they make sense to you now. Indeed, you can even appreciate the benefits of their lenses . . . and borrow them sometimes.

Now you can speak their language. And if they don't speak yours, please consider buying them a copy of this book.

# ACKNOWLEDGMENTS

We are enormously grateful to the many friends and colleagues who have helped us to develop, explore, and apply the principles of motivational focus and fit. This book would not have been possible without the Fellows of Columbia University's Motivation Science Center (once known, before it became an official "center," as simply the Higgins Lab)—particularly those who worked with us in the earlier years when motivational focus and fit were being developed: Tamar Avnet, Vanessa Bohns, Miguel Brendl, Jeff Brodscholl, Chris Camacho, Joe Cesario, Ellen Crowe, Jens Förster, Tony Freitas, Per Hedberg, Lorraine Chen Idson, Dan Molden, Nira Liberman, Jason Plaks, Chris Roney, Abigail Scholer, James Shah, Scott Spiegel, Tim Strauman, and Canny Zou.

We were fortunate to have the extraordinary Giles Anderson as our agent, friend, collaborator, and guide. *Focus* owes much to his vision, enthusiasm, and wisdom. We are deeply grateful for his contributions to the book.

We are also grateful for all the support and assistance we have received from everyone at Hudson Street Press and Penguin—particularly our superb editor Caroline Sutton. Caroline saw the diamond (we certainly hope it's a diamond) in the rough, and gave us much-needed clarity, in addition to a lot of very helpful and thoughtful feedback. The final product has benefited greatly from being in such capable hands.

Last, but naturally not least, we are both blessed to have the love and support of our brilliant and insightful family members, each of whom provided feedback on earlier drafts (and sometimes inspired our research, too)—Sigrid Grant, Jonathan Halvorson, Kayla Higgins, Jennifer Jonas, and Robin Wells.

# NOTES

## Introduction

1. Higgins, E. T. (1997). Beyond pleasure and pain. *American Psychologist*, 52, 1280–1300.

## Chapter 1: Focused on the Win, or Avoiding the Loss?

1. Keller, J. (2008). On the development of regulatory focus: The role of parenting styles. *European Journal of Social Psychology* 38, 354–64; E. T. Higgins (1991). Development of self-regulatory and self-evaluative processes: Costs, benefits, and tradeoffs. In M. R. Gunnar and L. A. Sroufe (Eds.), *The Minnesota symposia on child psychology*, Vol. 23, *Self processes and development* (pp. 125–65) (Hillsdale, NJ: Erlbaum); N. Manian, A. A. Papadakis, T. J. Strauman, and M. J. Essex (2006). The development of children's ideal and ought self-guides: Parenting, temperament, and individual differences in guide strength. *Journal of Personality* 74, 1619–45.
2. Manian, N., T. Strauman, and N. Denney (1998). Temperament, recalled parenting styles, and self-regulation: Testing the developmental postulates of self-discrepancy theory. *Journal of Personality and Social Psychology* 75, 1321–32.

3. Aaker, J. L., and A. Y. Lee (2001). I seek pleasures and we avoid pains: The role of self regulatory goals in information processing and persuasion. *Journal of Consumer Research* 28, 33–49.

4. Higgins, E. T., and O. Tykocinski (1992). Self-discrepancies and biographical memory: Personality and cognition at the level of psychological situation. *Journal of Personality and Social Psychology Bulletin* 18, 527–35.

5. Aaker and Lee, 2001.

6. Werth, L., and J. Förster (2006). How regulatory focus influences consumer behavior. *European Journal of Social Psychology* 36, 1–19.

7. Zhang, J., G. Craciun, and D. Shin (2010). When does electronic word-of-mouth matter? A study of product reviews. *Journal of Business Research* 63, 1336–41.

8. Fuglestad, P., A. J. Rothman, and R. W. Jeffery (2008). Getting there and hanging on: The effect of regulatory focus on performance in smoking and weight loss interventions. *Health Psychology* 27, S260–70.

9. Leonardelli, G. J., J. L. Lakin, and R. M. Arkin (2007). Regulatory focus, regulatory fit, and the search and consideration of choice alternatives. *Journal of Experimental Social Psychology* 43 (6), 1002–9.

## Chapter 2: Why Optimism Doesn't Work for (Defensive) Pessimists

1. Scheier, M. F., and C. S. Carver (1992). Effects of optimism on psychological and physical well-being: Theoretical overview and empirical update. *Cognitive Therapy and Research* 16 (2), 210–28.

2. Grant, H., and E. T. Higgins (2003). Optimism, promotion pride, and prevention pride as predictors of quality of life. *Personality and Social Psychology Bulletin* 29, 1521–32.

3. Norem, J., and E. Chang (2002). The positive psychology of negative thinking. *Journal of Clinical Psychology* 58 (9), 993–1001.

4. Higgins, E. T. (2012). *Beyond Pleasure and Pain: How Motivation Works* (London: Oxford University Press).

5. Sackett, A. M., and D. A. Armor (2012). Reasoned optimism: The "intuitive functionalist" account of personal predictions. Manuscript under review.

## Chapter 3: Focus on Work

1. Friedman, R. S., and J. Förster (2001). The effects of promotion and prevention cues on creativity. *Journal of Personality and Social Psychology* 81, 1001–13.
2. Rietzschel, E. (2011). Collective regulatory focus predicts specific aspects of team innovation. *Group Processes Intergroup Relations* 14, 337–45.
3. Rusetski, A., and L. Lim (2001). Not complacent but scared: Another look at the causes of strategic inertia among successful firms from a regulatory focus perspective. *Journal of Strategic Marketing* 19 (6), 501–16.
4. Herman, A., and R. Reiter-Palmon (2011). The effect of regulatory focus on idea generation and idea evaluation. *Psychology of Aesthetics, Creativity, and the Arts* 5, 13–20.
5. Förster, J., H. Grant, L. C. Idson, and E. T. Higgins (2001). Success/failure feedback, expectancies, and approach/avoidance motivation: How regulatory focus moderates classic relations. *Journal of Experimental Social Psychology* 37, 253–60.
6. Liberman, N., L. C. Idson, C. J. Camacho, and E. T. Higgins (1999). Promotion and prevention choices between stability and change. *Journal of Personality and Social Psychology* 77, 1135–45.
7. Brockner, J., E. T. Higgins, and M. Low (2003). Regulatory focus theory and the entrepreneurial process. *Journal of Business Venturing* 19, 203–20.
8. Wallace, J., L. Little, A. Hill, and J. Ridge (2010). CEO regulatory foci, environmental dynamism, and small firm performance. *Journal of Small Business Management* 48, 580–604.

## Chapter 4: Focus on Kids

1. Higgins, 1991.
2. Higgins, E. T. (1989). Continuities and discontinuities in self-regulatory and self-evaluative processes: A developmental theory relating self and affect. *Journal of Personality* 57, 407–44.
3. Manian, Strauman, and Denney, 1998.
4. Case, R. (1985). *Intellectual development: Birth to adulthood* (New York: Academic Press).

5. Harter, S. (1986). Cognitive-developmental processes in the integration of concepts about emotions and the self. *Social Cognition* 4, 119–51.

6. Van Hook, E., and E. T. Higgins (1988). Self-related problems beyond the self-concept: The motivational consequences of discrepant self-guides. *Journal of Personality and Social Psychology* 55, 625–33.

7. Leung, C. M., and S. F. Lam (2003). The effects of regulatory focus on teachers' classroom management strategies and emotional consequences. *Contemporary Educational Psychology* 28, 114–25.

## Chapter 5: Focus in Love

1. Molden, D. C., E. J. Finkel, S. E. Johnson, and P. Eastwick (2012). Promotion- or prevention-focused attention to and pursuit of potential romantic partners. Manuscript in preparation, Northwestern University.

2. Finkel, E. J., P. W. Eastwick, and J. Matthews (2007). Speed-dating as an invaluable tool for studying romantic attraction: A methodological primer. *Personal Relationships* 14, 149–66.

3. Berscheid, E., and W. Graziano (1979). The initiation of social relationships and interpersonal attraction. In R. L. Burgess and T. L. Huston (Eds.), *Social exchange in developing relationships* (pp. 31–60) (New York: Academic Press).

4. Molden, D. C., L. D. Olson, and G. L. Lucas (2012). Motivating the development and restoration of trust. Manuscript submitted for publication, Northwestern University.

5. Liu, H. (2011). Impact of regulatory focus on ambiguity aversion. *Journal of Behavioral Decision Making* 24, 412–30.

6. Downey, G., A. L. Freitas, B. Michaelis, and H. Khouri (1998). The self-fulfilling prophecy in close relationships: Rejection sensitivity and rejection by romantic partners. *Journal of Personality and Social Psychology* 75, 545–60.

7. Winterheld, H. A., and J. A. Simpson (2011). Seeking security or growth: A regulatory focus perspective on motivations in romantic relationships. *Journal of Personality and Social Psychology* 101, 935–54.

8. Rusbult, C. E., P. A. M. Van Lange (2003). Interdependence, interaction, and relationships. *Annual Review of Psychology* 54, 351–75.

9. Molden, D. C., and E. J. Finkel (2010). Motivations for promotion and prevention and the role of trust and commitment in interpersonal forgiveness. *Journal of Experimental Social Psychology 46*, 255–68.

10. Santelli, A. G., C. W. Struthers, and J. Eaton (2009). Fit to forgive: Exploring the interaction between regulatory focus, repentance, and forgiveness. *Journal of Personality and Social Psychology 96*, 381–94.

11. Righetti, F., C. E. Rusbult, and C. Finkenauer (2010). Regulatory focus and the Michelangelo phenomenon: How close partners promote one another's ideal selves. *Journal of Experimental Social Psychology 46*, 972–85.

12. Winterheld, H. A., and A. Simpson (2012). Social support and regulatory focus: A dyadic perspective. Manuscript in preparation, California State University, East Bay.

13. Molden, D. C., G. M. Lucas, E. J. Finkel, M. Kumashiro, and C. E. Rusbult (2009). Perceived support for promotion-focused and prevention-focused goals: Associations with well-being in unmarried and married couples. *Psychological Science 20,* 787–93.

14. Bohns, V. K., G. M. Lucas, D. C. Molden, E. J. Finkel, M. K. Coolsen, M. Kumashiro, C. E. Rusbult, and E. T. Higgins (2012). Opposites fit: Regulatory focus complementarity and relationship well-being. *Social Cognition* (in press).

## Chapter 6: Focus on Making Decisions

1. Lee, A., P. Keller, and B. Sternthal (2009). Value from regulatory construal fit: The persuasive impact of fit between consumer goals and message concreteness. *Journal of Consumer Research 36*, 735–47.

2. Semin, G. R., E. T. Higgins, L. G. de Montes, Y. Estourget, and J. F. Valencia (2005). Linguistic signatures of regulatory focus: How abstraction fits promotion more than prevention. *Journal of Personality and Social Psychology 89*, 36–45.

3. Liberman, Idson, Camacho, and Higgins, 1999.

4. Scholer, A. A., X. Zou, K. Fujita, S. J. Stroessner, and E. T. Higgins (2010). When risk-seeking becomes a motivational necessity. *Journal of Personality and Social Psychology 99*, 215–31.

5. Pham, M., and T. Avnet (2004). Ideals and oughts and the reliance on affect versus substance in persuasion. *Journal of Consumer Research 30*, 503–18.

6. Werth, L., and J. Förster (2007). The effects of regulatory focus on braking speed. *Journal of Applied Social Psychology 37,* 2764–87.

7. Described in E. T. Higgins (2002), How self-regulation creates distinct values: The case of promotion and prevention decision making, *Journal of Consumer Psychology 12,* 177–91.

8. Herzenstein, M., S. Posavac, and J. Brakus (2007). Adoption of new and really new products: The effects of self-regulation systems and risk salience. *Journal of Marketing Research 19,* 251–60.

9. Kirmani, A., and R. Zhu (2007). Vigilant against manipulation: The effect of regulatory focus on the use of persuasion knowledge. *Journal of Marketing Research* 19, 688–701.

## Chapter 7: Focus on Our World

1. Boldero, J., and E. Higgins (2011). Regulatory focus and political decision making: When people favor reform over the status quo. *Political Psychology* 32, 399–418.

2. Ibid.

3. Lucas, G. M., and D. C. Molden (2011). Motivating political preferences: Concerns with promotion and prevention as predictors of public policy attitudes. *Motivation and Emotion 35,* 151–64.

4. Dolinski, D., and M. Drogosz (2011). Regulatory fit and voting. *Journal of Applied Social Psychology 41,* 2673–88.

5. Pew Research Center (2006). *Attitudes toward immigration: In black and white. http://pewresearch.org/pubs/21/attitudes-toward-immigration-in-black-and-white.*

6. *Los Angeles Times* (2008). Latinos still the largest, fastest-growing minority. May 1.

7. Stern, Eliyahu. Don't fear Islamic Law in America. *New York Times* (September 2, 2011).

8. Oyserman, D., A. Uskul, N. Yoder, R. Nesse, and D. Williams (2007). Unfair treatment and self-regulatory focus. *Journal of Experimental Social Psychology* 43, 505–12.

9. Wilson, R. W., and A. W. Pusey (1982). Achievement motivation and small-business relationship patterns in Chinese society. In S. L. Greenblatt, R. W. Wilson, and A. A. Wilson (Eds.), *Social interaction in Chinese society* (pp.195–208) (New York: Praeger).

10. Aaker and Lee, 2001.

11. Zaal, M., C. Van Laar, T. Stahl, N. Ellemers, and B. Derks (2001). By any means necessary: The effects of regulatory focus and moral conviction on hostile and benevolent forms of collective action. *British Journal of Social Psychology* 50, 670–89.

12. Brebels, L., D. De Cremer, and C. Sedikides (2008). Retaliation as a response to procedural unfairness: A self-regulatory approach. *Journal of Personality and Social Psychology* 95, 1511–25.

13. Moreland, R. L., and S. Beach (1992). Exposure effects in the classroom: The development of affinity among students. *Journal of Experimental Social Psychology* 28, 255–76.

14. Shah, J. Y., P. C. Brazy, and E. T. Higgins (2004). Promoting us or preventing them: Regulatory focus and manifestations of intergroup bias. *Personality and Social Psychology Bulletin* 30, 433–46.

15. Phills, C., A. Santelli, K. Kawakami, C. Struthers, and E. T. Higgins (2011). Reducing implicit prejudice: Matching approach/avoidance strategies to contextual valence and regulatory focus. *Journal of Experimental Social Psychology* 47, 968–73.

16. Förster, J., E. T. Higgins, and L. Werth (2004). How threat from stereotype disconfirmation triggers self-defense. *Social Cognition* 22, 54–74.

## Chapter 8: Identifying and Changing Focus

1. Freund, A. M. (2006). Age-differential motivational consequences of optimization versus compensation focus in younger and older adults. *Psychology and Aging* 21, 240–52.

2. Finegold, D., S. Mohrman, and G. M. Spreitzer (2002). Age effects on the predictors of technical workers' commitment and willingness to turnover. *Journal of Organizational Behavior* 23, 655–74.

3. Unpublished Motivation Science Center survey.

4. Van Dijk, D., and A. N. Kluger (2010). Task type as a moderator of positive/negative feedback effects on motivation and performance: A regulatory focus perspective. *Journal of Organizational Behavior* 32:8, 1084–1105.

5. Plessner, H., C. Unkelbach, D. Memmert, A. Baltes, and A. Kolb (2009). Regulatory fit as a determinant of sport performance: How to succeed in a soccer penalty-shooting. *Psychology of Sport and Exercise 10*, 108–15.

6. Van Stekelenburg, J., and B. Klandermans (2003). *Regulatory focus meten met behulp van spreekwoorden* [Using proverbs to measure regulatory focus]. *Jaarboek Sociale Psychologie* (Groningen, The Netherlands).

7. Van-Dijk and Kluger, 2004.

8. Florack, A., M. Scarabis, and S. Gosejohann (2005). Regulatory focus and consumer information processing. In F. R. Kardes, P. M. Herr, and J. Nantel (Eds.), *Applying social cognition to consumer-focused strategy* (pp. 235–63) (Mahwah, NJ: Lawrence Erlbaum Associates).

9. Aaker and Lee, 2001.

10. Sung and Choi, 2011. Increasing power and preventing pain: The moderating role of self-construal in advertising message framing. *Journal of Advertising*, 40, 71–86.

11. Shah, J. (2003). The motivational looking glass: How significant others implicitly affect goal appraisals. *Journal of Personality and Social Psychology* 85, 424–39.

12. Levine, J. M., E. T. Higgins, and H.-S. Choi (2000). Development of strategic norms in groups. *Organizational Behavior and Human Decision Processes* 82, 88–101.

13. Faddegon, K., D. Scheepers, and N. Ellemers (2008). If we have the will, there will be a way: Regulatory focus as a group identity. *European Journal of Social Psychology* 38, 880–95.

## Chapter 9: It's the Fit That Counts

1. Higgins, E. T. (2000). Making a good decision: Value from fit. *American Psychologist* 55, 1217–30.

2. Higgins, E. T. (2006). Value from hedonic experience *and* engagement. *Psychological Review* 113(3), 439–60.

3. Cesario, J., H. Grant, and E. T. Higgins (2004). Regulatory fit and persuasion: Transfer from "feeling right." *Journal of Personality and Social Psychology* 86, 338–404.

4. Avnet, T., D. Laufer, and E. T. Higgins (2012). Are all experiences of fit created equal? Two paths to persuasion. Manuscript submitted for publication, Columbia University.

5. Lee, A. Y., and J. L. Aaker (2004). Bringing the frame into focus: The influence of regulatory fit on processing fluency and persuasion. *Journal of Personality and Social Psychology* 86, 205–18.

6. Wang, J., and A. Y. Lee (2006). The role of regulatory focus in preference construction. *Journal of Marketing Research* 43(1), 28–38. doi:10.1509/jmkr. 43.1.28.

7. Aaker and Lee, 2001.

8. Paine, J. W. (2009). Follower engagement, commitment, and favor toward change: Examining the role of regulatory fit. Unpublished doctoral dissertation, Columbia University.

9. Li, A., J. Evans, M. Christian, S. Gilliland, E. Kausel, and J. Stein (2011). The effects of managerial regulatory fit priming on reactions to explanations. *Organizational Behavior and Human Decision Processes* 115, 268–82.

## Chapter 10: The Triumph of the Fittest

1. Lockwood, P., C. H. Jordan, and Z. Kunda (2002). Motivation by positive or negative role models: Regulatory focus determines who will best inspire us. *Journal of Personality and Social Psychology* 83, 854–64.

2. Schokker, M., J. Keers, J. Bouma, T. Links, R. Sanderman, B. Wolffenbuttel, and M. Hagedoorn (2010). The impact of social comparison information on motivation in patients with diabetes as a function of regulatory focus and self-efficacy. *Health Psychology* 29, 438–45.

3. Freitas, A. L., N. Liberman, and E. T. Higgins (2002). Regulatory fit and resisting temptation during goal pursuit. *Journal of Experimental Social Psychology* 38, 291–98.

4. *Wall Street Journal* (2010). BP links safety to pay in fourth quarter. October 19.

5. Daryanto, A., K. de Ruyter, and M. Wetzels (2010). Getting a discount or sharing the cost: The influence of regulatory fit on consumer response to service pricing schemes. *Journal of Service Research* 13, 153–67.

6. Brodscholl, J. C., H. Kober, and E. T. Higgins (2007). Strategies of self-regulation in goal attainment versus goal maintenance. *European Journal of Social Psychology* 37, 628–48.

7. Plessner, Unkelbach, Memmert, Baltes, and Kolb, 2009.

8. Unkelbach, C., H. Plessner, and D. Memmert (2009). "Fit" in sports: Self-regulation and athletic performances. In J. Forgas, R. Baumeister, and

D. Tice (Eds.), *The psychology of self-regulation* (pp. 93–105) (New York: Psychology Press).

9. Latimer, A. E., S. E. Rivers, T. A. Rench, N. A. Katulak, A. Hicks, J. K. Hodorowski, E. T. Higgins, and P. Salovey (2008). A field experiment testing the utility of regulatory fit messages for promoting physical activity. *Journal of Experimental Social Psychology 44*, 826–32.

10. Spiegel, S., H. Grant, and E. T. Higgins (2004). How regulatory fit enhances motivational strength during goal pursuit. *European Journal of Social Psychology 39*, 39–54.

11. Spiegel, Grant, and Higgins, 2004.

12. See Freitas, A., and E. T. Higgins, 2002. Enjoying goal directed-action: The role of regulatory fit. *Psychological Science 13*, 1–6.

13. Hamstra, M., N. Van Yperen, B. Wisse, and K. Sassenberg (2011). Transformational-transactional leadership styles and followers' regulatory focus. *Journal of Personnel Psychology 10*, 182–86.

14. Van-Dijk and Kluger, 2004.

## Chapter 11: Under the Influence

1. Zhao, G., and C. Pechmann (2007). The impact of regulatory focus on adolescents' response to antismoking advertising campaigns. *Journal of Marketing Research 19*, 671–87.

2. Aaker and Lee, 2001.

3. Cesario, Grant, and Higgins, 2004.

4. Holler, M., E. Hoelzl, E. Kirchler, S. Leder, and L. Mannetti (2008). Framing of information on the use of public finances, regulatory fit of recipients and tax compliance. *Journal of Economic Psychology 29*, 597–611.

## Chapter 12: To Market

1. Lee and Aaker, 2004.

2. Florack, A., and M. Scarabis (2006). How advertising claims affect brand preferences and category–brand associations: The role of regulatory fit. *Psychology and Marketing 23*, 741–55.

3. Lee and Aaker, 2004.

4. Lee, Keller, and Sternthal, 2009.

5. Wang and Lee, 2006.

6. Aaker and Lee, 2001.

7. Daryanto, de Ruyter, and Wetzels, 2010.

8. Uskul, A., D. Sherman, and J. Fitzgibbon (2008). The cultural congruency effect: Culture, regulatory focus, and the effectiveness of gain- vs. loss-framed health messages. *Journal of Experimental Social Psychology* 45, 535–41.

9. Higgins, E. T., L. C. Idson, A. L. Freitas, S. Spiegel, and D. C. Molden (2003). Transfer of value from fit. *Journal of Personality and Social Psychology 84*, 1140–53.

10. Mourali, M., and F. Pons (2009). Regulatory fit from attribute-based versus alternative-based processing in decision making. *Journal of Consumer Psychology 19*, 643–51.

11. Avnet, T., and E. T. Higgins (2003). Locomotion, assessment, and regulatory fit: Value transfer from "how" to "what." *Journal of Experimental Social Psychology 39*, 525–30.

12. Mourali and Pons, 2009.

## Chapter 13: A Step-by-Step Guide to Creating Motivational Fit

1. Förster, J., and E. T. Higgins (2005). How global versus local perception fits regulatory focus. *Psychological Science 16*, 631–36.

2. Semin, G. R., and K. Fiedler (1991). The linguistic category model, its bases, applications and range. In W. Stroebe and M. Hewstone (Eds.), *European review of social psychology*, Vol. 2 (pp. 1–50) (Chichester, England: Wiley).

3. Semin, Higgins, de Montes, Estourget, and Valencia, 2005.

4. Förster, Grant, Idson, and Higgins, 2001.

5. Grant and Higgins, 2003.

6. Förster, Grant, Idson, and Higgins, 2001.

7. Pennington, G. L., and N. J. Roese (2003). Regulatory focus and temporal perspective. *Journal of Experimental Social Psychology 39* (6), 563–76.

8. Avnet and Higgins, 2003.

9. Cesario, J., and E. T. Higgins (2008). Making message recipients "feel right": How nonverbal cues can increase persuasion. *Psychological Science 19*, 415–20.

10. Mourali and Pons, 2009.

11. Higgins, Idson, Freitas, Spiegel, and Molden, 2003.

12. Hong, J., and A. Y. Lee (2008). Be fit and be strong: Mastering self-regulation with regulatory fit. *Journal of Consumer Research 34*, 682–95; and Lee, Keller, and Sternthal, 2009.

13. Vaughn, L., A. Harkness, and E. Clark (2010). The effect of incidental experiences of regulatory fit on trust. *Personal Relationships 17*, 57–69.

14. Hong and Lee, 2008.

# INDEX

Note: Page numbers in *italics* indicate tables and illustrations.